Transclasses

Chantal Jaquet is a philosopher and professor at the University of Paris 1 Panthéon-Sorbonne. A specialist in the history of modern philosophy and the philosophy of the body, she is the author of twenty books on Spinoza, Bacon, and the body–mind relationship and olfaction.

Transclasses:

A Theory of Social Non-reproduction

Chantal Jaquet

Translated by Gregory Elliott

VERSO

London • New York

Cet ouvrage publié dans le cadre du programme d'aide à la publication
bénéficie du soutien du Ministère des Affaires Etrangères et du Service
Culturel de l'Ambassade de France représenté aux Etats-Unis.
This work received support from the French Ministry of Foreign
Affairs and the Cultural Services of the French Embassy in the
United States through their publishing assistance programme.

This work was published with the help of the French
Ministry of Culture – Centre national du livre
Ouvrage publié avec le concours du Ministère français
chargé de la culture – Centre national du livre

This English-language edition first published by Verso 2023
Translation © Gregory Elliott 2023
First published as *Les transclasses ou la non-reproduction*
© Presses Universitaires de France 2014

1 3 5 7 9 10 8 6 4 2

Verso
UK: 6 Meard Street, London W1F 0EG
US: 388 Atlantic Avenue, Brooklyn, NY 11217
versobooks.com

Verso is the imprint of New Left Books

ISBN-13: 978-1-83976-885-9
ISBN-13: 978-1-83976-887-3 (UK EBK)
ISBN-13: 978-1-83976-886-6 (US EBK)

British Library Cataloguing in Publication Data
A catalogue record for this book is available from the British Library

Library of Congress Cataloging-in-Publication Data
Names: Jaquet, Chantal, author. | Elliott, Gregory, translator.
Title: Transclasses : a theory of social non-reproduction / Chantal Jaquet
  ; translated by Gregory Elliott.
Other titles: Transclasses. English
Description: London ; New York : Verso, 2023. | "First published as Les
  transclasses ou la non-reproduction © Presses Universitaires de France
  2014"—Title page verso. | Includes bibliographical references and
  index.
Identifiers: LCCN 2022056865 (print) | LCCN 2022056866 (ebook) | ISBN
  9781839768859 (trade paperback) | ISBN 9781839768866 (ebook)
Subjects: LCSH: Social mobility—France. | Social stratification—France. |
  France—Social conditions.
Classification: LCC HN440.S65 J3613 2023 (print) | LCC HN440.S65 (ebook)
  | DDC —dc23/eng/20230126
LC record available at https://lccn.loc.gov/2022056865
LC ebook record available at https://lccn.loc.gov/2022056866

Typeset in Sabon MT by Hewer Text UK Ltd, Edinburgh
Printed and bound by CPI Group (UK) Ltd, Croydon CR0 4YY

To Renée Thomas, my aunt,
who crossed the Bonrieu for the first time.

To all transclasses

. . . this first world, which I shall leave
but which will not leave me.

Marie-Hélène Lafon

Contents

Introduction

Distinction within Distinction

In *The Inheritors* and *Reproduction*, Pierre Bourdieu and Jean-Claude Passeron examine how educational institutions perpetuate social hierarchy and domination.[1]

Although it caused a stir among idealists who believed in the virtues of emancipatory state education, the thesis has come to be widely known and accepted. The education system reproduces the existing order, on the one hand by ensuring that scions of the dominant classes obtain the best degrees and, cultural capital in hand, occupy the most advantageous social positions; on the other, by legitimizing academic ranking, the success or failure of individuals, by recourse to innate qualities and an ideology of 'giftedness' that transform social selection into penalty for personal deficiency.

Yet education represents just one of the cogs of reproduction. More generally, the process relies on handing down a familial and social legacy from one generation to the next. This inheritance does not boil down to the trio of material assets, knowledge, and power. Bourdieu bases his theory of reproduction on the transmission of four types of capital: economic capital, cultural capital, social capital, and symbolic capital. To the economic, cultural, and social resources conferred on individuals by wealth, theoretical or practical knowledge, and the

---

1 This book derives from a seminar conducted at the Sorbonne in 2010–11 and 2012–13. I would like to thank my students for giving me the strength to write it.

network of relationships imperative for acquiring social advantages, we must add all forms of capital (economic, cultural, social, and so on) that transform power relations into relations of meaning and produce symbolic effects by inducing others to acknowledge the legitimacy of the dominant position and to internalize their dominated status.

Reproduction relies not only on the institutions and procedures that favour and perpetuate it but also on shaping habitus through inculcating and conditioning conduct related to social class and individual conditions of existence. Habitus – an embodied system of acquired and enduring dispositions that generate representations and practices – thus emerges as the very lifeblood of reproduction. First defined by Bourdieu in *Outline of a Theory of Practice* in 1972, this key concept was continually reworked and refined thereafter.

In *The Logic of Practice* (1980), Bourdieu stresses how socialization leads individuals to incorporate rules of conduct and thinking in order to adapt to their conditions of existence. These rules will govern future conduct without necessarily being conscious or deliberately followed:

> The conditionings associated with a particular class of conditions of existence produce *habitus*, systems of durable, transposable dispositions, structured structures predisposed to function as structuring structures, that is, as principles which generate and organize practices and representations that can be objectively adapted to their outcomes without presupposing a conscious aiming at ends or an express mastery of the operations necessary in order to attain them. Objectively 'regulated' and 'regular' without being in any way the product of obedience to rules, they can be collectively orchestrated without being the product of the organizing action of a conductor.[2]

---

2 Pierre Bourdieu, *The Logic of Practice*, transl. Richard Nice (Stanford, CA: Stanford University Press, 1990), p. 53.

A reflection of the social world and lived experience, the habitus is the matrix of conduct; it governs strategies of individual action and defines a way of life based primarily on class distinction. Thus, no one is born a worker or a boss; one becomes such, from father to son . . . *or almost.*

In fact, the implacable logic of reproduction, whose mechanisms are rigorously analysed by Bourdieu and Passeron, leaves exceptional cases in the shadows. And not the least of the paradoxes is that its principal theorist eluded it in practice, since he freed himself (or was freed) from the constraints of the class he was born into. The son of a mail carrier (and, later, postmaster) and a mother from a peasant family, Bourdieu followed a social trajectory he was not predisposed to, given his origins. How do we explain that some individuals like him do not necessarily reproduce the conduct of their class, but pass from one class to another? Such anomalies remain a blind spot in the theory of reproduction, and the issue is how to account for them.

Remarkably, *Sketch for a Self-Analysis* does not ponder why Bourdieu did not reproduce the family model. Although he provides the keys for understanding his intellectual history and his focus on sociology instead of philosophy when admitted to the École Normale Supérieure and the *agrégation*, he does not look into the background factors contributing to his academic success and social ascent. Instead, his reflections begin with an analysis of the intellectual climate in Paris during the 1950s; the only biographical elements he includes are those required to explain his subsequent academic career.[3] His native social environment is only mentioned at the very end of the book, when discussing how certain dispositions associated with his origins helped determine his intellectual practice. If he alludes in snippets to his childhood and

---

3 Pierre Bourdieu, *Sketch for a Self-Analysis*, transl. Richard Nice (Cambridge: Polity, 2004), p. 9.

experience as a class defector (*transfuge*),[4] he never devotes sustained attention to why he excelled academically and enjoyed a social trajectory so different from the children of small-scale farmers, artisans, and tradesmen with whom he attended primary school, and whose circumstances, by his own account, he shared. Therewith, Bourdieu himself offers striking proof of *the need to conceive distinctions within distinction*. The question is how – failing a revolution or grass-roots collective reform movement – social non-reproduction is possible; and how to understand the singularity of exceptions in a process where things seem doomed to the repetition of the same.

Disgruntled people might think that Bourdieu deliberately obscures the issue because it casts doubt on his theory. This is not the case, since he himself allows for exceptions. While he rejects the idea of 'free will' with its train of voluntarist illusions, Bourdieu never regards reproduction as a matter of destiny or an iron law. Even if his position has often been misunderstood, his aim is not to encourage quietism or resignation, but to understand the forms of social determination in order to provide instruments for freeing ourselves from them. In *The Inheritors*, Bourdieu and Passeron are at pains to point out that social factors of class differentiation do not take the form of a mechanical determinism; and they consider two types of exception that confirm the rule of social reproduction.

In the first place, it would be unrealistic to think that cultural inheritance works in automatic, identical fashion for those who benefit from it.[5] In fact, there are two possible ways to use a legacy: by exploiting it or by squandering it.[6] Inheritors can make rational use of their cultural inheritance not only by

---

4 Ibid., p. 84.

5 Pierre Bourdieu and Jean-Claude Passeron, *The Inheritors: French Students and Their Relation to Culture*, transl. Richard Nice (Chicago: University of Chicago Press, 1979), p. 25.

6 Ibid., pp. 10–11, 25.

preserving it, but also by cultivating it with an ease and grace that break with mere laborious reproduction and express genuine creativity. Conversely, they can waste their cultural heritage, showing dilettantish attitudes in school or extravagant spending in society, leading eventually to their ruin.

Secondly, Bourdieu and Passeron observe that some children from disadvantaged backgrounds manage not to be eliminated in the educational selection process; they attribute this to greater adaptability to the exigencies of teaching and a supportive family environment. Even though the authors do not go into this phenomenon in depth, they encourage further research by emphasizing the 'need for more detailed study of the causes or reasons which govern these exceptional destinies'.[7]

That is why the logic of the theory of reproduction requires us to examine counterexamples to obtain a fuller understanding of their status and scope. The idea of non-reproduction must be carefully considered and merits closer attention, for the value and scope of 'non-' cannot be determined a priori.

In strictly logical terms, negation may express contradiction or contrariness. In the case of a contradictory opposition, reproduction and non-reproduction cannot coexist: consequently, if one is true, the other is necessarily false. Alternatively, in the case of a contrary opposition, the two theses are compatible. In short, the point is to find out whether an exception disproves or proves the rule. At stake in this inquiry are the nature of human power and the range of personal freedom. Non-reproduction brings into play the possibility of inventing a new mode of existence within an established order, in the absence of social upheaval or revolution.

It is not certain, in this respect, that this individual-level and quite exceptional phenomenon escapes the laws of reproduction or stands outside the social system. They can be a product of it

---

7 Ibid., p. 26. We will return to this point in Part I.

and help reinforce it by serving as a kind of safety valve. Alternatively, they can manifest liberty that has overcome the constraints of 'fate'. Either way, in the absence of in-depth examination we should abstain from any hasty conclusion that exceptions are dazzling proof of the falsity of the law of reproduction. The sociologist and philosopher Didier Eribon, for instance, although born into a working-class family, insists that his career cannot be interpreted as refuting social determinism. The existence of a few uncommon cases that do not prove the general rule is insufficient to invalidate the rule or deny its reality.[8] Eribon presents himself as a violator of the norm. But contravening the norm does not mean contradicting it. Instead, it prompts us to ask why, how, and to what extent such transgression is possible, given that no one can escape their past completely.[9]

In the absence of change on a collective scale, questions of the causes, means, and limits of individual non-reproduction are crucial. They are difficult to answer, for to date no comprehensive theory has been developed – and for good reason: obstacles are numerous and hinder efforts to conceptualize the issue. The timidity and conformism of researchers, who are more apt to create a following than dissidence, and to turn to subjects that have already been recognized and institutionally approved, would lead them more to explore forms of social reproduction – a necessary task if ever there was one – than to formulate a theory of non-reproduction, let alone one addressing marginal cases.

In this regard, the innovative approach taken by Bernard Lahire is welcome. Lahire has changed the scale of observation of social facts by looking at family particularisms among the popular classes. In his *Tableaux de famille* [Family portraits], he examines unlikely cases of children who

---

8 Didier Eribon, *Retours sur Retour à Reims* (Paris: Cartouche, 2011), p. 20.
9 Ibid., p. 19.

confound the low expectations bound up with the weak cultural capital of their class background not only by avoiding the risk of being left behind but by being at the top of their class.[10] To explain such anomalies in a homogeneous social environment, Lahire examines the family configurations, especially the domestic forms, of the written culture that reigns supreme in academic settings (reading stories aloud; reading newspapers, magazines, and books; making lists, plans, calculations, budgets; and so on). He includes parental moral codes and educational investments, birth order, and feelings of inferiority or importance, which play a decisive role in the formation and transmission of cultural capital. Admittedly, Lahire does not advance a theory of social non-reproduction, for the analysis treats what might be called non-reproduction in primary school. This type of non-reproduction cannot by itself explain social trajectories in adulthood, as it is true that the top students from the working class quickly join the ranks of 'murdered Mozarts' once they have to earn a living. All the same, Lahire's approach paves the way for a differential sociology by carefully examining diverse contexts and heterogeneous experiences.[11]

In contrast, most researchers avoid setting foot on the terrain of social non-reproduction. In their defence, it is worth pointing out that the subject is politically poisoned. The first obstacle is ideological in kind, and consists in the fact that the rare instances of social mobility are often brandished to conceal immobility and provide support for it. Individuals from the lower classes who climb the social ladder are used as mascots or symbols reinforcing the social order and fuelling

---

10 Bernard Lahire, *Tableaux de famille. Heurs et malheurs scolaires en milieux populaires* (Paris: Éditions du Seuil, 1995).

11 See also Bernard Lahire, *Portraits sociologiques, dispositions et variations individuelles* (Paris: Nathan, 2002), and *L'Homme pluriel* (Paris: Nathan, 1998). The latter is available in English as *The Plural Actor*, transl. David Fernbach (Cambridge: Polity, 2011).

the ideology of the self-made man. They serve as political showcases and alibis to reject collective demands and contain people's sense of injustice. Under these conditions, the point is not to go into the issue in more depth, for the answer has already been provided and boils down to the simple dictum: 'You can make it if you try hard enough.'

For their part, revolutionaries who want to change an unjust social order are disinclined to waste time on marginal phenomena, because, quite legitimately, their efforts focus on achieving collective and general non-reproduction. They prefer to leave exceptions unexamined in order to avoid encouraging individualism and to mobilize the masses effectively. In their eyes, the problem of non-reproduction in isolation risks looking like a second-order, compromised subject, a smokescreen deployed by the wealthy.

Yet there are probably lessons to be drawn from an examination of the causes of a profound change in the most unfavourable conditions, however individual and limited it may be. The most intensely progressive political thinker who, following a thoroughgoing revolution, has witnessed the same system reassert itself in spite of the fact that the people in charge have changed, would be making a grave mistake to disregard such micro-phenomena. He must understand the cluster of causes that enable individuals to transform themselves and not repeat the behaviours of their class, in order to prevent a revolution from bringing back the old ways under the guise of the new. Exceptional cases provide a vantage point for identifying the decisive factors in real change. Anyone dreaming of better days, then, has every reason to consider actual cases of transformation in a disenchanted world.

To remove this initial obstacle, it is first necessary to neutralize the problem, because the point is not to overestimate or downplay exceptions for political ends, but to understand them. It would be appropriate to refer to them objectively by subsuming them under a concept without any evaluative connotations. Indeed, we should note that, circumlocutions aside, no rigorous term exists for precisely naming those who do not reproduce the model of their social class. Social mobility is commonly described by means of spatial metaphors of movement upwards and downwards, which frequently contain a moral charge. Depending on its direction, it is described as promotion or, on the contrary, demotion.

Whatever its direction – rise or fall – social mobility is often cast in a critical and pejorative light. Accordingly, those who have left supposedly inferior social classes, and become 'respectable' (*embourgeoisés*), are called 'social climbers'; conversely, those who have been proletarianized, having lost status relative to their previous station in life, are social 'failures' (*déclassés*). But whether mocked or pitied, such individuals are not located in a conceptual framework. 'Class defector' is perhaps the least inadequate term, for it evokes the transfer that has been made. But it is not value-free, inasmuch as it connotes flight, desertion, and even treason. A defector is someone who has changed allegiance, trading one country or political party for another, and always falls under suspicion as a renegade.

This phenomenon is not unique to those who change class; it affects all those who do not reproduce the dominant model and discover their identity after being branded by an insult or taunt – unnamed because unnamable, like homosexuals stigmatized by defamatory epithets. Thus, the unspeakable homosexuality was most often referred to in abusive terms: 'faggot', 'queer', 'fairy', 'dyke', and so on, but also through denial or concealment by transfer of the practice to a place or person: 'lesbian' (a name that derives from the island of Lesbos), or 'sapphism' (from the poet Sappho). To be sure, *gay*, which was originally synonymous with 'happy', 'carefree', and 'cheerful', now counts as more positive and politically correct. In the course of the twentieth century, the term became the banner of homosexual self-worth, especially in demonstrations of 'gay pride' in the United States during the 1990s, when it expresses a carefree attitude with regard to conventional sexual mores. That said, the word *gay*, in its turn, is not entirely free of pejorative connotations. It was linked to immorality and debauchery as early as the seventeenth century. Although it did not expressly refer to homosexuality, it evoked lax moral attitudes. Thus, 'gay' might refer to a ladies' man; a 'gay' woman was a prostitute and a 'gay' establishment a brothel.[12]

To confer legitimate objective existence on those who do not reproduce the fate of their class of origin, it is therefore advisable to change terminology and invent a concept, rejecting pejorative language, whether metaphorical or normative. In this context, it would seem more prudent to speak of a *transclass* when referring to an individual who moves from one class to another, coining this neologism on the model of the term *transsexual*. The prefix *trans* does not suggest supersession or ascent, but merely transition, switching to another side. It is synonymous with the Latin word *trans*, which means 'across', and describes transit between two classes.[13] The real difficulty consists in conceptualizing the nature and origin of the *transitio* made by the transclass (plural: transclasses), which is at the heart of non-reproduction.

At this juncture, a second obstacle emerges, this time of an epistemological kind. The problem concerns the nature of an object that requires us to *think exceptions*. How can philosophy, which involves thinking in concepts, grasp singular cases

---

12 Although this meaning has been forgotten and replaced by positive connotations, it is worth noting that, at the precise moment the term *gay* underwent a revaluation in the United States, before being adopted across the world, it received a new pejorative charge in the English language (for example, the contemptuous remark for a bad idea: 'That's so gay'). In the same way, to call someone 'gay' meant calling him 'garbage'.

13 We will return to the justification of the term in due course. See 'Complexion as *Passing*' (Part II, p. 92).

and account for particularity? A *concept* is a means of gathering diverse elements and unifying them by synthesizing what they share with other cases of the same kind. Otherwise, they remain scattered in their multiplicity. Is it really possible to speculate about non-reproduction without getting lost in the clouds of abstraction or the swamps of empirical data? Can we fashion a concept of the individual in what is irreducible in him? Can we apprehend an inner essence, and capture freedom in its individual incarnation?

Spinoza's philosophy addresses this very problem, and his reflections have prompted a fair amount of ink to be spilled by commentators. Besides imaginative knowledge, which is inadequate, Spinoza lists two other kinds of knowledge that are adequate: 'knowledge of the second kind, or reason', which rests on common notions and ideas about the properties of things, without, however, revealing their essence; and 'knowledge of the third kind, or intuitive science', which is supposed to apprehend things in their singularity and to deduce their essence from that of God's attributes.[14] Such intuitive knowledge, which aims for the very idea of this or that human body and concerns the essence of singular things, is extremely arduous – so much so that many commentators deem it impossible, pointing out that Spinoza himself, at the very end of his *Ethics*, observes that the road to salvation consisting in knowledge of the third kind is 'as difficult as it is rare'.

Does this mean that the enterprise is doomed to failure from the outset? Is the very idea of a concept of the singular tantamount to a pure oxymoron? The challenge is to forge analytical tools for thinking the exception and understanding it philosophically. There is reason to fear that philosophy lacks the means to do so because, unlike the sociological method, it is not based on surveys and statistics. Consequently, we may

---

14 Benedict de Spinoza, *Ethics*, ed. and transl. Edwin Curley (London: Penguin, 1996), p. 57.

wonder whether the object in question is genuinely philosophical and whether the study of non-reproduction does not instead pertain to history or sociology.

Here, it must be noted that there are no objects that are inherently philosophical, while others are not. They are constituted as such by the invention of concepts, and are historical products that have emerged from an audacious expansion of reflection to include areas hitherto left fallow. Thinking does not observe borders any more than it has a sense of property. It scorns institutional divisions because it tackles new objects by devising new means of apprehending them. It is nourished by the natural sciences and literature alike, as well as by philosophy, history, and sociology. There is no private hunting ground or reserved domain a priori. For instance, the body represents an object for physics, biology, medicine, history, philosophy, and sociology in equal measure.

Although Bourdieu and Passeron have offered masterful reflections on reproduction and inheritance, this does not mean that sociology has a monopoly on the subject, as evidenced by Althusser's philosophical work on the topic.[15] What is more, if Bourdieu invokes a break with a certain philosophical tradition, he still derives concepts from it and reworks them in another field. When he allots a key role to the notion of habitus, he takes up the *hexis* of Plato's *Theaetetus* and Aristotle's *Nicomachean Ethics*, and assigns the term a new meaning.[16]

Sociology has its own field of competence and methods. But, like philosophy, it cannot set itself up as a hegemonic science and bar its doors to interdisciplinary contributions. As regards non-reproduction, sociology encounters difficulties comparable to those of philosophy. Thus, statistical inquiries

---

15 See Louis Althusser, *On the Reproduction of Capitalism: Ideology and Ideological State Apparatuses*, transl. G. M. Goshgarian (London/New York: Verso, 2014).

16 Aristotle, *Nicomachean Ethics*, Book II, Chapter 3, 1105a, 30.

prove unavailing when the cases under observation are not analogous. Non-reproduction concerns exceptional cases, and, if one compares such cases to class or to regroup them on the assumption that they are similar, one will be inclined to privilege similarities and erase particularities, so that conclusions risk being fallacious. Consequently, methodological tools different from those traditionally employed must be fashioned.

This is what Norbert Elias did in *Mozart: Portrait of a Genius*, which affords here a model for philosophical thought. The study grasps the irreducible singularity of Mozart, his peculiar genius, which led him not to follow in the footsteps of his father – a court musician – but to abandon the petty bourgeoisie and achieve prominence as a creative artist moving in aristocratic circles. Elias's method involves focusing on a singular case, examining its social constraints, and noting elements of the historical and artistic context that shed light on the subject: the courtly milieu, the status of artists from lower social strata, oppositions between aristocratic and bourgeois norms, canons of taste and musical invention, and so forth.

However, Elias does not set out to write a historical biography or to dwell on Mozart's particular fortunes. Rather, the aim is to construct a model capable of shedding light on the conditions governing the artistic condition at this point in history. As the author puts it, 'such a study is not a historical narrative but the elaboration of a verifiable theoretical model of the figuration which a person – in this case an eighteenth-century artist – formed through his interdependence with other social figures of his time.'[17] Although Elias's focus is not non-reproduction, he shows through Mozart's example that it is possible to conceptualize it, and he foils the presumption of impossibility attached to thinking about the singular.

---

17 Norbert Elias, *Mozart: Portrait of a Genius*, transl. Edmund Jephcott (Cambridge: Polity, 1994), p. 14.

The task, then, is to elaborate a model of the transclass and to sketch a theory of non-reproduction by employing not only philosophical concepts but also intellectual tools borrowed from other areas, which likewise enable us to grasp the singular in a universal light. Above all, reflections will draw on literary fictions that afford examples of non-reproduction – for instance, the story of Julien Sorel in Stendhal's *The Red and the Black*. Philosophy cannot do without literature, which furnishes an array of experiences and hypotheses whose richness and detail are often overlooked. Thus, Didier Eribon has observed that fiction offers as many resources as sociology or more theoretical books for grasping the diversity of individual and collective experience in the social universe. Moreover, he makes extensive use of literature in order to understand his own career.[18] The speculation here will also be based on autobiographical narratives by transclasses that combine literary discourse and theoretical reflection – for example, *Black Boy* by Richard Wright and *Brothers and Keepers* by John Egdar Wideman.

However, rather than novels or autobiographies in the strict sense, auto-socio-biographical accounts will be privileged – for instance, writings by Annie Ernaux, Didier Eribon, and Richard Hoggart – which seek to think the life or destiny of an individual in relation to their environment, as a social product and not as the coming-of-age of a self cut off from any external determination.[19] Thus, Ernaux has stated that her three books – *A Man's Place*, *A Woman's Story*, and *Shame* – 'are

18   Eribon, *Retours sur Retour à Reims*, p. 42.
19   See especially Annie Ernaux, *A Man's Place*, transl. Tanya Leslie (New York: Ballantine Books, 1992), originally published as *La Place* (Paris: Gallimard, 1983), and *Shame*, transl. Tanya Leslie (New York: Seven Stories, 1998), originally published as *La Honte* (Paris: Gallimard 1987); Didier Eribon, *Returning to Reims*, transl. Michael Lucey (London: Penguin, 2019); Richard Hoggart, *A Local Habitation: Life and Times, 1918–1940* (London: Chatto & Windus, 1988).

not autobiographical so much as auto-socio-biographical'.[20] Unlike autobiography, which tends to impose the reductive image of authors speaking about themselves, the auto-socio-biographical practice of writing takes the form of a story where the point is not so much rediscovering the self as losing it in a larger reality: a common condition or shared social suffering.[21] In this context, the seeming gap between the singularity of the exception and the universality of the concept recedes, since the whole human condition is expressed, and a situational anthropology delineated, through the individual. Ernaux ventures an explanation by hypothesizing that the more personal a text is, the more universal it can become, probably because it expresses an intimate experience in which readers can recognize themselves, going beyond the variety and particularity of individual life-stories.[22]

Eribon's approach, which occupies a middle ground between Bourdieu's self-analysis and Ernaux's socio-biography, is also very enlightening. In recounting his personal experience, Eribon aims to render the exemplary story of a child from the working classes whose educational and social trajectory gradually removes him from his class of origin.[23] Although he draws on his own trajectory, he does not present *Returning to Reims* as an autobiography but as a theoretical analysis of the social world rooted in a singular lived experience.[24] While the analysis is born of personal experience, it also sheds new light on it and attests to the reciprocal relationship between theory and individual history.

Starting from these various resources, my aim is to think the origin and condition of the transclass not in sociological terms,

---

20 Annie Ernaux, *L'Écriture comme un couteau* (Paris: Stock, 2003), p. 20.

21 Ibid., p. 21.

22 Ibid., p. 153.

23 Eribon, *Retours sur Retour à Reims*, p. 40.

24 Ibid.

or in an auto-socio-biographical account, but philosophically, by endeavouring to develop concepts that make it possible to apprehend the phenomenon. My analysis will focus on social non-reproduction, and more specifically on the transition from the world of the dominated to that of the dominant, which seems more of a mystery than the converse scenario. The causes of social *déclassement*, while varied (natural disasters, social upheavals, family bankruptcy, rupture or conflict, personal political decision, and so on), are easier to picture. This does not prevent us from considering the potentially two-way direction of translation; nor does it imply some primacy of social non-reproduction over other forms of non-reproduction (biological, sexual, racial, gendered). Non-reproduction is not restricted to the social mobility of transclasses. It can also manifest itself in renunciation, voluntary or otherwise, of the dominant model of propagating the species, of heterosexual norms, of the condition imposed on a race or sex. Consequently, we shall have to consider the imbrication of all forms of non-reproduction to solve the mystery of the emergence of transclasses in spite of everything – despite the curses of race, sex, and class.

Part I
The Causes of Non-reproduction

Society being divided by rings like those on a bamboo cane, everyone's chief preoccupation is to climb into the class above his own, and the whole effort of that class goes into stopping him from rising.

Stendhal, *Memoirs of an Egotist*

Transclasses who experience a meteoric social rise often elicit admiration that masks profound incomprehension. They are fascinating and inspire others to dream because they seem to have escaped, to be prodigies, beating the odds and defying reason. They give magical thinking something to fix on, for their fabulous destiny has something miraculous about it. Their exceptional career seems to elude rational explanation, and it gives rise to a veritable mythology of giftedness, luck or merit. In turn, this mythology nourishes the ideology of personal success, the belief at the heart of the American Dream: anyone born in the United States or emigrating there can grow rich and prosper, starting out with nothing, thanks to fortitude, will-power, and hard work.

But, whether we hail genius, imagine that some are born under a lucky star, or proclaim that they pulled themselves up by their bootstraps, the trajectory of transclasses remains incomprehensible when cloaked in clichéd formulas and metaphors that stand in for concepts. Indeed, these pseudo-explanations are the asylum of ignorance – worse even, perfidy – in that they lend themselves to stigmatization and political recuperation. Does it mean indeed that the vast majority of those who never rise above their initial station are stupid, unlucky, or lazy?

Instead of invoking good fortune or good nature, we should view the transclass phenomenon in terms of necessity, divesting it of any moral and political second thought. That is why analysing the causes of non-reproduction is the first essential task. Failing an understanding of their origins, exceptional destinies provide a ready alibi for moralism, lending credence to the idea that everyone bears full responsibility for their lot in life, and for conservatism, fuelling the conviction that the social order reflects the intrinsic merits of each person and rightly punishes laziness or stupidity.

Ambition, Queen of Non-reproduction?

The first reason generally advanced to explain exceptional cases is the presence in them of ambition, which expresses itself in the form of will-power and energy directed towards a single aim: success and social ascent, with its procession of honours. This ambition is voiced as a challenge, as when Eugène de Rastignac calls out upon his arrival in Paris: 'It's between you and me now' (À nous deux maintenant). For Balzac's hero, it is a matter of defying destiny, freeing himself from his origins, and distinguishing himself by transforming what might crush him into a powerful lever. Far from representing a hindrance, his energy is fuelled by the difficulty of the undertaking. The bigger the obstacle, the greater the young man's desire to overcome it. Paradoxically, then, the coefficient of adversity in things turns into its opposite, disadvantage into advantage: whatever seems banal and uninteresting to blasé, bourgeois eyes will only burn more brightly and fire the ardour of the worker's son. Bourdieu remarks this very process in a brief aside on the exceptional cases of non-reproduction: if individuals hailing from disadvantaged classes will most probably reproduce the original model, it would not be difficult to show that some of them, albeit few in number, will view their patent handicap as a challenge, mustering all the energy they can to free themselves from their social fate and rise above the common lot.[1]

Fed by a desire for distinction and grandeur, ambition acts as the motor of non-reproduction and social ascent. The two heroes created by Balzac and Stendhal, Eugène de Rastignac and Julien Sorel, are exemplary in this regard. Ambition sweeps aside all the scruples and fears that might still tie Julien Sorel to his native milieu. It leads him to renounce the liberty and security of the provincial petty bourgeoisie, deemed paltry and mediocre, and propel himself centre-stage in the world. Under the sway of this passion, hopes of a great but uncertain good eclipse any fear of losing a small but certain good. This is revealed by an exchange that occurs when Julien, dismissing the objections of his friend Fouqué, who points out the perils of all-consuming ambition, is about to reach Paris and enter the service of Marquis de la Mole. Prophetically, Fouqué predicts that the young man's career will end badly, and that he will hear of him via the shame attaching to the name Sorel. He tries to get the reckless youth to recognize that he is rushing to his financial and moral doom. For it is better to earn 100 louis trading lumber as one's own boss than to engage in unseemly, vile intrigue to obtain a government position that may pay 4,000 francs but entails being the lackey of the powerful. Julien refuses to listen. So happy to go up to Paris and make a splash in Paris at the marquis's side, he considers his friend's advice a form of small-mindedness: the view of the timorous provincial bourgeois fearful of surrendering a bird in the hand for two in the bush.[2]

Indeed, for Stendhal, ambition does not fuel personal

---

1   Pierre Bourdieu and Jean-Claude Passeron, *The Inheritors: French Students and Their Relation to Culture*, transl. Richard Nice (Chicago: University of Chicago Press, 1979), pp. 25–6.

2   Stendhal, *The Red and the Black*, transl. Catherine Slater (Oxford: Oxford University Press, 1991), p. 224.

careerism alone. It is at work throughout history and constitutes a principle of action and social transformation, as is indicated by the conversation Julien overhears between two travellers whose paths cross as one of them is getting out of a
carriage and the other getting in:

> The history of England offers me a mirror for our future.
> There'll always be a king trying to increase his prerogative; the
> wealthy inhabitants of the provinces will always be kept awake
> at night by the ambition to be elected to the Chamber of
> Deputies and by the fame and hundreds of thousands of francs
> earned by Mirabeau: they'll call this being liberal and caring
> about the people. The wish to become a peer or a gentleman of
> the Chamber will always spur on the ultras.[3]

Ambition rules the world and seems to be a permanent anthropological given. Far from being a rare phenomenon, it affects
all social strata and prompts them to seek to rise to the higher
level and obtain the best positions. In *Leviathan*, Hobbes
identified it with '*Desire* of Office, or precedence'.[4] Precedence,
by definition, is the right to take one's place before others and
to sit higher than them in the hierarchy. Thus, on the ship of
state, everyone aspires to hold the wheel, as Stendhal recalls;
and there is no room for the simple passenger.[5] Under the
impetus of ambition, the logic of attainment triumphs, so that
anyone intent on staying put passes for a halfwit.

Ambition aims at self-promotion and is fuelled by emulat-
ing others. The spring of ambition is the desire to surpass
oneself and to shift places in order to occupy the front rank
and lead the pack. Viewed from this angle, paradoxically,

---

3 Ibid., p. 240.
4 Thomas Hobbes, *Leviathan*, ed. Richard Tuck (Cambridge:
Cambridge University Press, 2013), p. 41. Emphasis in original.
5 Stendhal, *The Red and the Black*, p. 240.

non-reproduction is the rule and reproduction the exception, since it is a question not of people conforming to their original position, or consolidating it, but reaching a higher sphere – becoming a deputy, becoming a gentleman, becoming king and enhancing one's prerogatives when one is king. In its essence, ambition obeys a principle of indefinite increase and accumulation. It impels human beings to conquer and to go one better, so that the summit is, in its turn, merely the base of a podium to be reached.

That is why Spinoza defines it as 'an excessive desire for esteem'.[6] Esteem, which is the joy produced by the fact that someone rightly or wrongly believes themselves lauded for their actions, is the motive underlying the conduct of the ambitious.[7] Ambition is based on an intense desire for praise and distinction, leading individuals to emerge from obscurity to create a name for themselves and distinguish themselves in the admiring eyes of others. It can therefore legitimately be invoked as an explanatory hypothesis for non-reproduction, since it involves rejection of the prevailing conformism – what Nietzsche called 'herd morality' – in favour of the quest for an exceptional destiny. And it is precisely the excessive, over-abundant character of the energy at work in ambition that makes it possible to understand how the individual finds the strength to free herself from her native milieu and overcome obstacles. The immoderation it attests to is an integral part of its nature and efficacy. Consequently, it should not necessarily be seen as a vice.

In fact, ambition is not systematically synonymous with social climbing and careerism. In itself, it is simply the expression of a desire to live and to affirm one's power of acting. It is neither good nor bad inherently, but can be blamed or

---

6 Benedict de Spinoza, *Ethics*, ed. and transl. Edwin Curley (London: Penguin, 1996), p. 111.

7 Ibid., p. 109.

praised depending on the ends aimed at and the means employed. The objective is therefore to criticize it not from an ethical perspective, but from an epistemological standpoint, for the issue is whether it represents a wholly satisfying explanatory principle.

Here there are legitimate grounds for doubts. For, if ambition triumphing over obstacles and resistance appears as one of the keys to non-reproduction, it remains to explain why the appetite for life and self-assertion that manifests itself in it is not to be found in all human beings. Not everyone has the appetite of an Alexander or a Caesar. How does it come about that some people are ambitious, while others are not? If ambition is an explanatory principle for exceptions, how are we to explain that, as a general rule, human beings tend to reproduce the lifestyle of their social class? Does it come down to saying that the latter tendency is bound up with a lack of ambition?

Such an explanation would be rather limited, for it assumes that ambition is a natural given, a form of psychological determination constitutive of the personality, a character trait at the root of human behaviour. On the basis of these premises, lack of ambition appears either as a natural defect, attributable to an ontological inequality between human beings, or as a character defect attributable to subjects themselves, who make poor use of their freedom and volition in aiming for mediocre, humdrum objectives. It would then be quite easy to conclude that social reproduction is due to a natural fatality or moral failure on the part of individuals, and to account for it by recourse to the ideology of giftedness or merit.

Such a conclusion would be fallacious, for ambition is not a given and cannot be conceived as a first cause. Like any affect, it is one of the forms that can be taken by individuals' power of acting, and it is explained by specific causes. If based on a desire for esteem and energy deployed to that end, the question is why the power of acting takes this form. Why is it that energy prevails over inertia and is freed in the service of this objective and not some other? Ambition is not so much constitutive as constituted.

In effect, whether social or economic, intellectual, or artistic, any ambition is ambition *for* something and presupposes the idea of a model, an ideal, a goal to be achieved. In the case of non-reproduction, it involves the representation of a model other than the dominant one, and the existence of a desire to realize it. In other words, ambition is not the first cause, but the effect of a process that combines cognitive determination – the idea of a model, even if confused – and affective determination: the desire to accomplish it. To believe that ambition is at the root of non-reproduction is to confuse an effect with a cause. If ambition is ambition for something, this something has to have emerged to make it possible.

That is why, when the ambitious person is depicted in the guise of a 'self-made man', a misleading portrait is painted, for he has not made himself out of nothing, like some miraculous creation *ex nihilo*. Thus, to say of a man that he is 'self-made' is to speak without saying anything, for we are not shown what he made himself from. Those who reply that, by definition, the self-made man made himself *out of himself* fall into a vicious circle, positing in advance the *himself* whose formation or constitution they are seeking to explain. A mask for ignorance, ambition plays the role of an occult quality that simply covers with a name a reality whose causes remain concealed. It is merely an apparent cause, not the ultimate reason for non-reproduction. The visible part of the iceberg, it must be attached to its hidden part in order for the phenomenon to be grasped as a whole. For, in the absence of the latter, it is severed from its premises and remains unintelligible.

Models and Imitation

The precondition for any ambition is the representation of a real or imaginary model that the individual desires to realize. Thus, there is no ambition without imitation. In this sense, all non-reproduction is a form of reproduction, because it involves imitating a model other than the dominant model in one's class of origin. How could Julien Sorel have come to desire a destiny other than that of peasant, carpenter, or wood merchant, if he had not had before him models different from that embodied by his father and his fellows? Julien's ambition is initially born out of the Napoleonic model. From childhood, he dreams excitedly that he will one day be presented to the most beautiful women in Paris and delightedly caresses the possibility of being loved by one of them, as Bonaparte, a simple soldier without any fortune, was by the brilliant Madame de Beauharnais. The obscure lieutenant become emperor is the prototype of social success via conquest, amorous as well as military. For many years, Stendhal tells us, not an hour of his life went by without Julien telling himself that Bonaparte 'had made himself master of the globe with his sword'.[8]

Julien's fascination with Napoleon is fed by reading of accounts of the *grande armée* and the *Memorial of Saint Helena*, which is his favourite book.[9] It goes beyond imaginary compensation to engender genuinely mimetic conduct, as attested by the adoption of the emperor's bodily gestures at Monsieur Chélan's. During a dinner of priests at which Julien gives a eulogy of Napoleon, he holds his right arm against his stomach, pretending to have dislocated it while shifting a tree trunk, and will keep it in this uncomfortable position for two months.[10]

---

8 Stendhal, *The Red and the Black*, p. 26.
9 Ibid., p. 22.
10 Ibid., p. 27.

From Napoleon, Julien retains not the sword, but social ascent via women. Madame de Rénal is his Joséphine, Mathilde de la Mole his Marie-Louise. Not coups d'état, but grand gestures to seduce; the Bible is his imperial army. For the foil, he substitutes the flower of Latin letters; for having hesitated between the red and the black, he renounces the scarlet uniform of the hussar for sombre ecclesiastical dress. The wind of history has turned: France is no longer threatened with invasion; military merit and the prestige of arms are out of fashion; and the salary of a forty-year-old priest is three times higher than that of Napoleon's famous major-generals. There will be no procrastinating: priest it is.[11] Julien stops talking about Napoleon and embraces the more lucrative career of priest. Accordingly, Bonapartist military imitation gives way to clerical imitation. Julien strives to imitate the model of the perfect abbot; he studies his facial expressions and postures to reproduce them faithfully. He firstly practises attaining the condition of *non culpa*. But, despite his efforts, he finds it difficult to assume the pious appearance of the seminarian submitting to religious faith and, after several months of trying, still has the air of thinking: 'What endless trouble he took to attain that facial expression of fervent and blind faith, ready to believe and suffer anything, that is so often encountered in monasteries in Italy . . .'[12]

However, Stendhal's novel offers an example of deliberate imitation that should not be generalized, unless it is thought that non-reproduction always derives from a free decision and obeys a form of voluntarism. In fact, most of the time, the imitation that governs behaviour occurs unbeknown to actors, and pertains not so much to a conscious decree as to an automatic process. This is what Spinoza brings out when he describes the phenomenon of imitation of the affects in the

---

11 Ibid.
12 Ibid., p. 191.

Ethics.[13] Experience shows that children, for example, start to laugh or cry solely because they see others behaving thus; and, more generally, that they imitate everything they see done by others spontaneously and quite unthinkingly. This stems from the fact that their young bodies are, as it were, in a state of equilibrium: they are highly malleable, not as yet stamped by fixed habits, so that they are open to different postures.

Thus, in the absence of any reason for laughing or crying, the child reproduces without any deliberation the behaviour of one of its fellows whose inner motives escape it. This infantile imitation is not the effect of a will or a mental process. It is constructed out of images and reflections derived from viewing bodies and their similarity. What is the reason for this? It derives from the fact that the human body is affected by external bodies, bears their traces or images, and is disposed to reproduce them. For Spinoza, the cause of this is that 'the images of things are the very affections of the human body, *or* modes by which the human body is affected by external causes, and disposed to do this or that.'[14] Imitation is the consequence of a corporeal determination that is not systematically conscious. When it takes root in infancy, it pertains more to reflex than reflection. Imitation of the affects and conduct in a given class or milieu is therefore non-intentional in essence. It is even likely that most of the time it results from an imitative corporeal schema, rather than a deliberate choice or a conscious learning process.

But whether imitation is conscious or not does not fundamentally alter the terms of the problem, for in both instances the question arises of how an individual can imitate a model which is not that of their native milieu. Indeed, if, as a general rule, individuals are destined to reproduce the dominant model, it is difficult to understand how they can imitate

---

13 Spinoza, *Ethics*, p. 87.
14 Ibid. Emphasis in original.

examples other than those they have before them, and which have a lasting effect on them. How can there be an imitation of non-reproduction? The antinomy is patent. It would be necessary to be able to picture or imitate an exceptional destiny, but how can one picture or imitate what escapes the general rule?

The family model

To account for particular cases that escape the iron law of reproduction, Bourdieu and Passeron venture an explanatory hypothesis that plays a particular factor in the family background off against the general law of the social milieu.[15] To this end, the two sociologists rely on noting an anomaly: the objective chances of acceding to higher education being forty times stronger for the son of a senior executive than the son of a worker, we should find the same proportion between the average number of individuals on university courses from working-class families and the families of senior executives. 'We find that, among a group of medical students, the average number of members of the extended family who are or have been in higher education varies in the ratio of only *one to four* between working-class students and upper-class students.'[16] Thus, the rare students from disadvantaged classes on university courses differ from other individuals from their background by virtue of the presence of a relative (or several relatives) in the family circle who has risen socially. This cultural situation is special, in as much as the existence of close or distant relatives who have studied at university fosters a stronger subjective hope of going to university among other family members. In this case, ignorance of the objective chances of succeeding becomes a factor in success. At least,

---

15 Bourdieu and Passeron, *Inheritors*, pp. 25–6.
16 Ibid., p. 26. Emphasis in original.

such is the explanatory hypothesis advanced by Bourdieu and Passeron, subject to verification: intuitively calculating their educational chances on the basis of the success of family members, and unaware of the actual statistics, they surmount a sizeable obstacle, for they are not led to resign themselves in advance and abandon higher education as something impossible for people from their category.[17]

No doubt, things turn out here as in games of chance or the lottery, where the near certainty of losing that should logically deter players is magically forgotten once one sees a neighbour or family member win. The phenomenon of identification with the winner thus works in favour of the wager, and the conduct of the player, which might resemble magical, irrational behaviour, is in fact a form of imitation. But, rather than the model of fellow losers, it follows the example of the winner with whom the individual identifies all the more strongly, in that she desires it intensely and is prompted to do so by ties of kinship. Thus, paradoxically, a certain form of ignorance and self-blindness lies behind exceptional destinies, whereas lucidity would lead people to abandon university studies so as to avoid inevitable failure. In this sense, as Spinoza observed, even a vain hope can be conducive to the power of acting.

Yet this does not mean that those who do not set about changing their condition are victims of their caution and err through an unduly rational attitude. In fact, the overwhelming majority of individuals from the popular classes who do not go to university do not do so in full knowledge of the facts, following deliberate reflection on failure and success rates. A vague awareness of their appointed lot in life transpires in the famous formula often found in the mouths of the sons and daughters of workers: 'that's not for the likes of us'. But self-elimination is the result not so much of a

---

17 See ibid., pp. 26–7.

deliberate choice as of a complex process where social selection takes the insidious form of discouragement, lack of motivation, and anticipation of failure that leads to not passing the examination.

Although not further developed, Bourdieu's explanation has the merit of not limiting the issue of reproduction to a phenomenon strictly bound up with social background, and of revealing the existence of a network of causality pertaining to family background. It thus paves the way for research into particular family circumstances and mitigates the potentially reductionist dimension of the concept of social class. But it remains incomplete and problematic because it leaves two fundamental questions hanging. Firstly, supposing that familial imitation is the determining cause of non-reproduction, how are we to explain the fact that a first relative escaped it in the absence of any model among relatives? Secondly, if the person who eludes the logic of self-censorship does so because a close or distant relative was upwardly mobile, how are we to explain the fact that, within the same family, two children, raised in similar fashion and with the same model of social promotion before them, do not have the same exceptional destiny, and that one continues studies while the other does not?

The first problem goes beyond the framework of family history, for it is more generally related to the paradox of beginning and the possibility of an inaugural non-reproduction. To resolve it, we must go into the specific details of a history and try to understand how, absent familial or social precedents, an individual can free herself from her condition and escape reproduction. Here the itinerary of the writer Annie Ernaux, hailing from a modest family that owned a small café-grocery in Yvetot, is particularly instructive. For it discloses an exemplary case of non-reproduction in the absence of antecedents. This story is the prototype of the singular universal contained in literature, from which philosophy should draw inspiration if it wishes to understand exceptions to reproduction. In *Shame*, Ernaux analyses her childhood universe and its secret sea-change in the episode, soon over, when her father sought to kill her mother. To such an extent does the world of the café-grocery impose itself as the only reality that her initial description of it highlights the difficulty, impossibility even, of escaping reproduction. Thus, she confesses: 'At the age of twelve I was living by the rules and codes of this world; it never occurred to me that there might be others.'[18]

Ernaux's world is made up of a stratification of rules and codes that convey 'a sense of confinement' and function as 'Tables of the Law'.[19] More precisely, it obeys three sets of legislation interlinking the general mores of the *quartier*, the precepts of petty commerce, and the imperatives of Catholic private schooling. In the first instance, young Annie is subject to the rules of living common to the clientele that gravitates around the small grocery-café in Yvetot. These are rules of surveillance, first of all. They are concerned with both 'teaching' children and spying on adults, endeavouring to know everything about other people's lives while revealing as little as possible about one's own. They also present themselves as principles of categorization and assessment of beings in accordance with a type of sociability based on simplicity, candour, and politeness. This involves appreciating 'good folk', who take an interest in other people, and condemning those who live apart, like bears or savages, refusing invitations, not returning favours, and taking no notice of anyone. Finally, these rules answer to a requirement of conformity and uniformity, where the ideal is to be like everyone else and exclude eccentricity, to the point where all the dogs in the

---

18 Annie Ernaux, *Shame*, transl. Tanya Leslie (New York: Seven Stories Press, 1998), p. 51.

19 Ibid., pp. 57–8.

quartier are called either Rover or Spot.[20] In this closed sphere, an eccentric is regarded as mentally deranged.

Grafted onto the communal ethic, secondly, are the particular rules of the café-grocery, defining the ethos peculiar to the good shopkeeper who, on account of constant exposure to the public gaze, has to behave respectably, control emotions of anger or sorrow, and avoid arousing envy by displaying wealth. This second stratum, which Ernaux defines as the 'code of behavior of the perfect storekeeper', involves a specific form of politeness, comprising discretion, modesty, and restraint, so as not to lose customers and go out of business.[21] For little Annie, it entails learning to say hello to customers in a clear voice, to greet them first, not to spread gossip or malicious remarks, never to reveal the family income, never to boast or put on airs and graces.[22]

Above all, however, the world of the Catholic private school, marked by the indissoluble union of two duties – believing and knowing – is what dominates her existence and leaves the deepest traces in her body and mind.[23] Life there is punctuated not only by prayer, catechism, and observance of the religious practices that seems more important than knowledge but also by a strict discipline governing bodily postures: lining up and going to classes in silence; getting up and remaining standing in the presence of the mistress before being invited to sit; inclining one's head, eyes, and body when speaking to her or encountering her; refraining from going to the toilet other than in break time, and so forth.[24]

Annie Ernaux's world is thus made up of habitus that do not predispose her to an exceptional destiny, since what prevails in it is an ideal of conformity and obedience to rules

---

20 Ibid., pp. 51, 56.
21 Ibid., p. 57.
22 Ibid.
23 Ibid., p. 61.
24 Ibid., p. 67.

so strongly internalized that they seem as eternal as natural laws. This is what clearly emerges from *Shame*:

> I feel compelled to use the present tense to list and describe these rules, as if they have remained as immutable as they were for me at the time. The more I explore this world of the past, the more dismayed I am by its coherence and its strength. Yet I am sure I was perfectly happy there and could aspire to nothing better.[25]

It is to be noted that not only does Ernaux not imagine another world but, above all, does not desire a different one. In this respect, her situation is analogous to that of the prisoners in the cave described by Plato in Book VII of the *Republic*. Obviously, the allegory of the cave does not describe social mobility: it paints a picture of the character of human beings according to whether it is enlightened by education or not. Nevertheless, it helps us understand the transition from ignorance to culture and the conditions for changing worlds. Like the prisoners in the cave who have no view other than the shadows projected onto the inside of the wall facing them, Annie Ernaux's story supports the idea that human beings who live in a given social condition have no representations of the world apart from those obtaining in their milieu.[26] They cannot imagine the existence of a different world and their desires are confined to this closed universe. So how might they escape it?

No doubt, it could be objected that the allegory is a fiction and that Ernaux's case could not happen today, for with the

---

25   Ibid., p. 68.

26   This is confirmed by Richard Hoggart in *A Local Habitation: Life and Times, 1918–1940* (London: Chatto & Windus, 1988): 'We had virtually no lines out to lives, interests, concerns, beyond ourselves. This was not innate selfishness or self-absorption; these were the terms, the ground-plan of our lives forced on us by the stringency with which our mother had to operate' (p. 38).

THE CAUSES OF NON-REPRODUCTION

existence of modern means of information (newspapers, tele-
vision, the internet) diffusing alternative images on a grand
scale, individuals have an abundance of lifestyle choices. But it
would be wrong to think that the presence of other models is
sufficient to impel individuals to deviate from the initial
schema. In the existence of the prisoners in the cave, there is
no room for critique, for imagination, or the desire for an
elsewhere, since their world is the real world. Plato stresses
this forcefully: 'what people in this situation would take for
truth would be nothing more than the shadows of the manu-
factured objects.'[27] And even when he has emerged from the
cave into the presence of the true reality, which dazzles him, a
freed prisoner would be highly embarrassed and 'believe the
things he saw before to be more true than what was being
pointed out to him now'.[28]

Ernaux is not saying anything different. Should she be
confronted with a different world – that of the secular state
school – which might offer her an alternative, it does not
appear catholic to her in the strong sense of the term. It is a
world in negative, without mass or prayer, full of errors and
darkness, in contrast to the world of truth and light in which
she moves. An unnameable world, or at any rate rarely named:
the word *secular* rings out like blasphemy, and for her vaguely
resembles something bad.[29]

Consequently, the presence of another world, which might
disturb the initial coherence, simply strengthens it at the
outset, so strong is the influence of common representations,
or what is appropriately called the dominant ideology. Any
other world will be rejected as one of falsity or sin. To believe
that it is enough to display life models in a shop window for

27 Plato, *The Republic*, ed. G. R. F. Ferrari, transl. Tom Griffith
(Cambridge: Cambridge University Press, 2015), p. 221.
28 Ibid.
29 Ernaux, *Shame*, p. 69.

customers to be enticed, and to adopt those life models as one takes clothes off the peg and tries them on, is to ignore the formidable power of ideology, which can extend as far as yielding an outright inversion of values. The prisoners in the cave afford a striking example of this: the illusory seems real to them, and reality illusory.

How, then, to escape a world that generates all its own conditions of reproduction? Even when it is possible to escape it, the issue is how. Saving oneself without any outside help is unthinkable, for it is impossible to conceive an existence of which one does not have the slightest idea. Non-reproduction does not occur via spontaneous generation. In the allegory of the cave, the prisoners do not emerge spontaneously, but are freed by force. But who is the mysterious 'one' who enters the cave and releases the men chained to their fate? Initially evasive, Plato subsequently informs us that the task of deliverance falls to the philosopher educated by society, who must go back down into the cave to pay his debt and educate other men. However, the original question always returns. How was the first philosopher able to escape? In the case to hand, non-reproduction is manifestly based on external aid. Well may the cave be opened, but one does not emerge alone. If there is no 'first parent' to stimulate the imaginary, we must assume the existence of other models to imitate.

The educational model

Family figures aside, the first exemplary imago with which an individual can identify is the schoolmaster or schoolmistress. Thus, in countries with a public education system, the educational model plays a key role, affording an alternative to the dominant familial and social model. Although schooling unquestionably contributes to social reproduction via selection and the elimination of disadvantaged social classes, in many cases it plays a liberating, emancipatory role. Such is the paradox of an institution that is worked on from within by its contradictions: it produces both the perpetuation of the system and its contestation by dint of the multitude and diversity of its singular agents, who are irreducible to mere transmission belts.

Thus, Richard Hoggart salutes the devotion and missionary spirit of certain teachers, characterized by their sense of responsibility, pedagogical and social alike, particularly towards intelligent pupils from families where no one has previously been to grammar school.[30] However critical he may be of schooling, Bourdieu himself stresses the fact that the adolescent, trainee student, seeking to make and create herself, draws inspiration from the role models and masters of thought found in the intellectual world, and very often in the teaching body with which she has most contact during her studies.[31] He recognizes that 'every student's academic path is crossed by some "great professor"'.[32]

Even though, in France, the campaign for secular, free and compulsory schooling, which followed the implementation of Jules Ferry's legislation, has sometimes pertained more to myth than reality, we must underscore the fundamental role of those who have been called the 'hussars of the republic', who offered a model of success or alternative values to boys and girls from disadvantaged classes. Once, in villages, the male or female teacher used to appear like a notable, affording a first image of the scholar and the intellectual. The fact that these hussars were recruited and selected partly from among the best pupils of the popular classes encouraged all the more identification with their image, in that they knew the native milieu well and could be recognized by it.

---

30 Hoggart, *Local Habitation*, p. 167.
31 Bourdieu and Passeron, *Inheritors*, p. 40–1.
32 Ibid., p. 41.

Although Annie Ernaux was not a pupil in the secular public sector, she owed her salvation partly to a teacher, Mademoiselle L., a nun in civilian dress who would help free her from her world by embodying a desirable model of excellence and perfection. Yet, judging from the almost caricatural portrait of the strict teacher given of her, there was nothing likeable about Mademoiselle L. Small, thin, ageless, with a grey bun and spectacles like magnifying glasses, she had a reputation for terror among parents and pupils alike. But the young Annie did not ask herself if she liked her or not; she knew no one around her who was so educated, and discovered in her a female figure different from her mother's customers or her aunts, the 'living embodiment of authority' who 'could guarantee the excellence of my scholastic being every time I reeled off a poem or handed in a faultless dictation'.[33]

Mademoiselle L. thus introduced a form of alterity into an undifferentiated, homogeneously female milieu. Through her teaching and her rigour, she offered an image of a superior female capable of endowing little Annie with another being, freeing her from her identity as a simple shopkeeper's daughter. She was the objective guarantor of an 'educated' possibility, a warrant of perfection acquired through schoolwork, since her judgement infallibly distinguished the good pupil from the bad by separating the true from the false. She was thus the living figure of the law, which rewards or punishes, defining hierarchies that did not necessarily reproduce the established social order. In and through recognition of her academic excellence, Annie Ernaux conducted an experiment in distinction; she felt her alterity, ceasing to be a pupil like all the others and rising to the rank of mistress, in a logic of connivance and identity. Thus, when Mademoiselle L. corrected her, it was not to humiliate her but to communicate her perfection to her; when she prevented her from

---

33 Ernaux, *Shame*, p. 76.

responding so as to allow others the time to hit upon the answer, or asked her to explain a logical analysis to them, she positioned Annie alongside her.[34] Symbolically, the good pupil who is held back is already on the side of the teacher and can see her fellow pupils in difficulty from the height of her pedestal. If she is prey to social shame, the posture of having been chosen is a source of narcissistic satisfaction and revenge against her lot, which she doubtless scarcely wants to give up for her entire life. Ernaux confesses that, in this world promoting academic success, she enjoyed recognition of her excellence, the freedom and privileges earned by coming first.[35] We can understand then why school is everything for her, as noted by those around her; and why this decisive experience is a motor of non-reproduction all the more powerful for encountering no opposition from her family, where the mother is presented as a relay of religious and educational rules.[36]

In cases of extreme poverty, where education is only episodic, the model of the teacher or intellectual likewise remains a reference and a life raft, as shown by Richard Wright in *Black Boy*. Born in 1908 in Natchez, Mississippi, where a very violent form of racial segregation prevailed, young Richard was doomed to a life of poverty and submission, like most of the blacks who shared his existence. He experienced hunger pangs, as his father, night porter in a drug store, had abandoned his family, leaving it penniless. Employed in the house of white people, his mother often took him to work along with his brother to prevent them getting up to mischief.

---

34   Ibid., p. 76.
35   Ibid., p. 74.
36   Ibid., p. 84. Ernaux does not confine her mother to this role, for she offered her a different model from that of the housewife. She also signals in *L'Écriture comme un couteau* (Paris: Stock, 2003) the crucial influence of a teacher in her final year at lycée, Madame Berthier, in her career and her political awareness (p. 70). Over and above the educational model, she mentions her discovery of the work of de Beauvoir and then of Bourdieu.

Richard Wright, his stomach empty, watched the whites eat in sullen anger. When, by chance, they left something, he fed off their leftovers. Otherwise, he and his brother had to make do with tea and bread.[37] Yet Richard would become a famous writer, the first great black American novelist, who paved the way for authors like James Baldwin or Chester Himes. This idea of being a writer was obviously not seeded by his family: his strictly Puritan grandmother even forbade him to read novels, regarding them as sources of perdition. Still less was it instilled by the whites by whom he was employed. Far from it – they did everything to humiliate him and put him in his place, as attested by the dialogue between the young Richard and his female boss, whose brutality enables us to understand the extent to which, for a black kid, the desire to be a writer is an anomaly, even a scandal. When she asks him why he needs to go to school, and he timidly dares to say that he would like to become a writer, he receives a scathing reply: '"You'll never be a writer," she said. "Who on earth put such ideas into your nigger head?"'[38]

If such a fanciful idea has been able to germinate in this 'nigger head', it is in part thanks to the desire and love of literature that Ella, a young black teacher boarding with is grandmother, awakened in the little Richard Wright by reading him the story of *Bluebeard* despite the family ban. This silent, distant young lady, who at once attracts him and scares him, opens the gates of 'a forbidden and enchanting land' populated by words buzzing with plots, murders, and passions.[39] This wider world, which sharpens his perception and expands his imagination, bursts into his narrow, drab existence. Thereafter he is forever stealing books, learning to decipher them in secret, bombarding his mother with

37 Richard Wright, *Black Boy* (London: Vintage, 2020 [1945]), p. 17.
38 Ibid., p. 147.
39 Ibid., p. 38.

questions to decode the meaning of unknown words: 'I had tasted what to me was life, and I would have more of it, somehow, someway.'[40]

No doubt we are dealing with a romanticized view of the birth of a literary vocation, with its share of retrospective illusion in describing the exaltation of a subject discovering the existence of an entrancing elsewhere. However, the author is not fooled, but recreates the past emotion while suggesting in the background that the underlying cause of his desire to read was in the first instance perhaps desire for a female reader. Desire for a female reader in several senses: desire for Ella reading, desire of Ella so that he reads, or again desire to be read by Ella, and so on. The unwitting or forgotten imitation of beginnings: a necessary stage in reappropriating a desire and making oneself its deliberate author?

While a large number of authors of novels or intellectual autobiographies mention the crucial role of teachers or professors in their trajectory of social non-reproduction, the educational model is not a panacea.[41] Imitation is a necessary, but insufficient, condition. For every Annie Ernaux or Richard Wright, how many Jude the Obscures gave up en route in spite of all their efforts to free themselves from their insecure condition?

---

40 Ibid.

41 See, for example, James Baldwin, *Notes of a Native Son* (London: Penguin, 2017 [1955]), pp. 92–4. The son of a Harlem minister, James Baldwin, who lived in very considerable poverty with his eight brothers and sisters, stresses the importance for his family and for him of a very generous young, white, female schoolteacher, who took an interest in him, lent him books, and took him to the theatre. See also Hoggart, *A Local Habitation*, which highlights his debt to his school teachers, especially the headmaster, Mr Harrison, 'who gave me a leg up at the right time far beyond their calls of duty', as a result of which he went on to grammar school – but especially Bonamy Dobrée, an enthralling professor of English literature, who acted as 'an intellectual father figure' for him at Leeds University (pp. 154, 217).

The Socio-economic Conditions of Non-reproduction

It would be a mistake to think that non-reproduction is entirely bound up with the existence of intellectual figures and educational models imitated by individuals who identify with them in a kind of transference, and who follow their example in order to make their own way. In fact, it rests on economic and political conditions – in particular, the establishment of a programme of instruction for all in free, secular, compulsory schools, in tandem with a system of substantial bursaries, without which further and higher education are the preserve of inheritors. Michel Étiévent also stresses the decisive role of works councils in the world of labour, which offer bursaries to disadvantaged children to continue with their education: 'I owe everything to the factory works council. As a child, I read thanks to its library, I went on holiday thanks to its summer camps, I stayed on at school thanks to its education bursaries.'[42] In the absence of institutions or financial resources, the thirst for knowledge very often becomes the misfortune of being unable to quench it.

In France, for example, the model of the hussars of the republic could only become a motor of non-reproduction because it was inscribed in the institutional framework of the *écoles normales* for male and female teachers, which had to recruit the teachers required for the mandatory schooling of children in each department. Abolished under the Vichy regime, these *écoles normales*, following their restoration in 1945, made it possible to select the best pupils from the popular classes and train an elite by financing extended periods of study. The social elevator operated especially after the Second World War, when the recruitment competition for teachers was directed at Year 10 pupils in the complementary courses of the 'popular' curriculum, by contrast with the 'bourgeois'

---

42 Michel Étiévent, *Fils d'usine* (Paris: Éditions Gap, 2005), p. 133.

curriculum of lycée pupils. Successful candidates in this exacting competition embarked on training in the *écoles normales* where, all expenses paid, over four years they studied for the baccalauréat and then the teachers' vocational qualification. In addition, these *écoles normales* offered the best trainee teachers opportunities for internal promotion to the *écoles normales supérieures* and to secondary-level teaching.

The first possibility, which already existed under the Third Republic, was to advance via fourth-year competition to special classes preparing for the entrance examination for the École Normale Supérieure of Saint-Cloud for boys, or that of Fontenay-aux-Roses for girls, to become a teacher and then the headmaster of an *école normale primaire* or an inspector of primary.

Starting with the Fourth Republic, the second opportunity for promotion consisted in awarding a bursary to the best pupils in the second year to take their third year in one of the two regional classes carefully selected by the administrative centre, pursuing either the '*bac math-élem*' (the elementary mathematics baccalauréat) for those good at mathematics, physics, and chemistry, or the '*bac philo*' (the philosophy baccalauréat) for those good at humanities. After obtaining the baccalauréat, and depending on the final ranking drawn up by the teachers' committee, these pupils could either join a preparatory class at the École Normale Supérieure of Saint-Cloud for boys, or that of Fontenay-aux-Roses for girls, or be assigned to a training centre to become college teachers, or return to their original *école normale*.

A third possibility was made available to the pupils of *écoles normales* at the end of their baccalauréat or after their fourth year: obtaining a scholarship to train as a PECG (general college teaching professor). At the same time, these pupils could enrol at university and take the competitive Preparatory Institutes for Secondary School Teaching exam, where they were paid for three years to pursue the secondary school teaching diploma, and then the *agrégation* or a master's degree (DES), which allowed them to become a lycée teacher or head of an institution, or to pursue a career in the private sector. Finally, *école normale* pupils excelling at gymnastics could take the competitive exam for entry into the Regional Institutes for Physical Education and Sport and, after three years' education, become PE teachers – in some cases entering the École Normale Supérieure d'Éducation Physique et Sportive.[43]

The *écoles normales primaires* played a decisive role in non-reproduction, not only because they offered unprecedented financial resources by assuming responsibility for studies from the second year of lycée, with boarding paid and a clothing grant, but because they provided a conducive institutional educational framework where pupils were taken out of their native milieu to benefit from a specific cultural and pedagogical environment focused on training them to the highest level and to succeed. Indeed, breaking through economic barriers by way of bursaries, wages, or grants is not enough to escape social reproduction. The sociocultural barriers that prevent pupils from popular strata believing in their own abilities must also be overcome, and suitably intensive teaching provided. In this respect, it is highly instructive to note that when, after 1970, trainee teachers from the popular classes, who at the end of Year 10 had passed the competitive exam for entry into the *école normale*, ceased to be assigned to their *écoles normales* to pursue the baccalauréat, and were sent to lycées where they mixed with the whole student cohort, without enjoying closer supervision, their success rates in the entry competition for the Écoles Normales Supérieures of Saint-Cloud and Fontenay-aux-Roses fell significantly five years

---

43 For more details, see Alain Vincent, *Des hussards de la République aux professeurs des écoles – L'École Normale* (Joué-lès-Tours: Éditions Alan Sutton, 2001); André Payan-Passeron, *Quelle École and quels enseignants? Métamorphoses françaises sur trois générations à partir des 34 Normaliens d'Avignon* (Paris: L'Harmattan, 2006).

later, even though there had been no reduction in financial support. And when financial support was reduced with the abolition of the entry competition for the *école normale* in Year 10, and its relocation post-baccalauréat, on the one hand, and the abolition of the Institut de Préparation aux Enseignements de Second Degré in 1978, on the other, social mobility began to decline seriously.

To identify more clearly the role played by institutions like the *écoles normales* for teachers, abolished in 1991 in favour of teacher training institutes, and assess through them the determinant character of socio-economic conditions for non-reproduction, there is no need to multiply examples. One will suffice: the destiny of a small village in Savoy over three generations following the Second World War. This mountain hamlet, whose population in the past thirty years has varied between eighty and fifty, was inhabited by very poor small breeders – sometimes peasants who worked at the neighbouring factory or the mine or, later, seasonal workers in the ski resorts. Living conditions were very harsh. Thirteen hundred metres up, wheat does not grow and the earth, steeply sloping, has to be raised every year to the summit of the field or garden with the help of stretchers. The craggy, small meadows can only be harvested, with difficulty, using motorized engines, and the cow herds rarely exceed a dozen.

Yet this village – whose inhabitants lived from 1945 to 1975 on an income often below (or barely equal to) the minimum wage, in great destitution and, in some cases, lacking any comforts, not even running water at home – counts, out of the thirty pupils who completed their education in this period, seven who succeeded in the entry competition for the *école normale* for teachers in Savoy (three girls, four boys), and an eighth who became a gymnastics teacher after having passed the CREPS.[44]

---

44 Editor's note: Regional Committee for Physical Education and Sports.

Of the seven teachers, four – two boys, two girls – gained admission to the École Normale Supérieure of Saint-Cloud or Fontenay-aux-Roses in the philosophy section. Of the four former pupils of the ENS, three were philosophy *agrégés*, while the last changed direction after 1968 and lives today from his writing. Among the three philosophy *agrégés*, who are lycée teachers – two women, one man – one has become a professor in preparatory classes in Paris, while another has a philosophy doctorate and has become a professor at the Sorbonne. In short: out of fifty inhabitants, three teachers, four *normaliens*, three of them graduate professors of philosophy and one a PE professor.

This microphenomenon has earned the hamlet's inhabitants a reputation in surrounding villages for being 'intellectuals who set the world to rights'. This is encapsulated in the ritual formula – a mixture of admiration and derision – that accompanies the revelation of their place of residence: 'Ah, you're from the university of T . . .!'

When the inhabitants are asked the reasons for this exceptional destiny, the first thing that comes unanimously to mind is the influential role of Mademoiselle G., a single, childless teacher held in high esteem and respected for her ability, devotion, and generosity, who spent her whole career in this harsh village blocked by winter snows. It is probably no accident if, under the thumb of this model hussar, the first two pupils to succeed in the entry competition for the *école normale primaire* were girls, and if, ultimately, it was one of them and her niece who got furthest in their studies. These two pioneers were followed by four boys, their brother, and cousins, and then in the subsequent generation by the niece and nephew of one of them trained by a new teacher, Mademoiselle R.

But if the educational model and the family model are combined, mutually reinforcing one another, it must be noted that this model would have remained utterly ineffectual without the bursary system in place. For, in the previous generation, the parents and older sisters of these trainee teachers could not, despite their admiration for their teacher, strong desire to learn, and excellent results, pursue their studies beyond the school certificate for want of financial means. As regards subsequent generations, when the primary school closed in the 1970s, and the few children from the village had to go to school in the neighbouring village, there was no longer any social mobility. This was down to the disappearance of a favourable teaching framework in a single class with small numbers, on the one hand, and the abolition of the entrance competition for the *école normale* in Year 10, on the other. The last pupil from the village admitted to the competition for the *école normale* in Year 10 dates back to 1973.

Although the educational model, coupled with adequate economic and pedagogical arrangements, can work, it cannot be systematically regarded as the key to non-reproduction. It can apply to very good pupils, but, by definition, excellence is the exception. There is only one first place, or two tied for first at a pinch, but what to make of the cohort of those coming next? Success is not in the reach of all and, in general, the educational experience of children from the popular classes is one more of failure than success. The education system is seen less as a tool of liberation through culture than as a system of repression. The sanction of the grade falls like a guillotine, and the social ladder very often seems like a scaffold.

The model of the charismatic teacher is therefore not universalizable – far from it. Even excellent pupils from the labouring classes do not end up identifying with it without feeling torn. Oscillating between model pupil and dunce, they challenge the educational order and are frequently insolent and disruptive. Talkative in class, Annie Ernaux confesses that she was neither diligent nor very studious, and that she cultivated a dunce-line and distracted side to live down her good grades and remain close to her fellow pupils. She thus had it both ways: seeming to be a bad pupil without being one, so as not to be shunned by the others, and remaining in the good graces of her teacher.[45]

In *Returning to Reims*, Didier Eribon also describes himself as 'an excellent student, but always on the verge of giving up on school altogether', and highlights the tension in very good pupils from the popular classes between social incapacity to abide by school disciplinary norms and a desire to learn.[46] This ambivalence towards school, which emerges from school reports in the form of assessments like 'good pupil but poor behaviour', does not, however, obey constitutive psychological determinations. It derives from a social situation, from an in-between posture where the subject is divided between a desire to succeed and the fear of betraying their class, or an inability to submit to a different order. As Eribon remarks, Bourdieu, though he forged the fertile concept of 'cleft habitus', probably does not go far enough in his *Sketch for a Self-Analysis* when he describes himself as an excellent pupil, but undisciplined and antagonistic.[47] He foregrounds explanations that pertain more to character psychology – personal idiosyncrasy – than to the logic of social forces at work in determining behaviour.[48]

Maladjustment to the educational order, with its train of discouragement and disobedience, yields the most effective selection there is: the self-elimination of pupils from the popular classes who sometimes make it a badge of honour to reject the system and leave before being expelled. Such maladjustment to the educational system, however, is not the preserve of pupils from the popular classes, but sometimes involves

---

45 Ernaux, *Shame*, p. 74.

46 Eribon, *Returning to Reims*, transl. Michael Lucey (London: Penguin, 2019), p. 153.

47 Bourdieu, *Sketch for a Self-Analysis*, transl. Richard Nice (Cambridge: Polity, 2004), pp. 96ff.

48 Eribon, *Returning to Reims*, pp. 154–5.

children from the big bourgeoisie, whose relationship to the language and culture is different from that governing the educated practice of teachers. Less marked by a spirit of seriousness, and impregnated since childhood with a culture of the humanities that it might seem vulgar to learn and hoard, they look like dilettantes and are penalized for a feigned laziness, which in reality is merely the expression of a class ethos that recoils from conspicuous scholarliness. Everyone recognizes their own, and it is unsurprising to find that the pupils who do best at school are the children of teachers.

Excellent pupils from the popular classes, for whom school is an opportunity, are forever walking a tightrope, divided between obeying school rules, which earns them the admiration of teachers, and indiscipline, which earns them the admiration of their peers. Two models of success: being a brainbox or being a dunce. We need to understand the logic that makes it possible to swing in one direction rather than the other, or to reconcile these contradictory desires.

Beyond the issue of how a thirst for learning can prevail over rejection, or hopes of success over fear of failing, the more general issue is determining why an individual identifies with a different model from that operative in their milieu. The presence of an alternative way of life is not sufficient to trigger a mechanism of non-reproduction. Certainly, children have a tendency to imitate unthinkingly, but unconscious, involuntary imitation is not enough to define a lasting orientation, for it does not necessarily have the capacity to establish itself in the face of opposing inclinations. We therefore need to understand the interplay of forces at work in adhesion to a model, be it familial or educational. This requires an analysis of what makes it desirable in action, uncovering the tangle of determinants that clash and compromise to produce a power of acting capable of bringing it about.

That is why it is important to think about the logic of the affects at work in non-reproduction. For it is not explained either by the existence of alternative models or by the establishment of political institutions and economic resources.

Affects and Encounters

Whatever their feeling of solitude, individuals are not entities that exist on their own, or doorless, windowless monads. They are relational beings constantly affected by external causes that modify them and which they alter in their encounters. To understand an individual is therefore to understand the dynamic constitution of their being in action through their affects. By affect, we do not mean a form of psychological determination or a character trait, but (following Spinoza) the set of physical and mental modifications that have an impact on the desire of each person, enhancing or reducing their power of action.[49] The affect refers to what touches us, motivates us, and moves us. It is the expression of an encounter between the causal power of an individual and that of the external world; and it refers both to what forms and fashions individuals, and to what they form and fashion, inasmuch as everyone is at once affecting and affected. Given that it is impossible to extricate ourselves entirely from the action of external causes, human beings are subject to a multiplicity of modifications and tossed about by contrary affects. The affect has its own kind of necessity: it does not obey the commands of reason and does not disappear by decree. Its power stems from external causes that continue to produce effects and leave traces.

---

49 Benedict de Spinoza, *Ethics*, ed. and transl. Edwin Curley (London: Penguin, 1996): 'By affect I understand affections of the body by which the body's power of acting is increased or diminished, aided, or restrained, and at the same time, the ideas of these affections. Therefore, if we be the adequate cause of any of these affections, I understand by the affect an action; otherwise, a passion' (p. 70).

48

That is why (so Spinoza tells us) 'an affect cannot be restrained or taken away, except by an affect opposite to, and stronger than, the affect to be restrained'.[50]

In the case to hand, we are seeking to understand the combination of affects that determine a child to assert, and bolster, a desire buffeted by contradictory forces, which impel the child both to remain within and to leave their native milieu – to be, like Eribon, an excellent pupil forever on the point of rejecting the educational institution. If the transition from one world to the other can be made in the face of all opposition, it is via affects that shore it up and counterbalance contrary forces. Before taking the form of a conscious, deliberate choice, the eruption of a sovereign desire is the result of underground work.

In the case of Didier Eribon, it is clear that identification with the cultural model embodied by the teaching body did not occur immediately and self-evidently. The switch from one world to another is largely made through an encounter, an affect, that will later be understood as being like amorous desire, but which to his thirteen-year-old adolescent eyes took the form of a bond of friendship with a young lad in his class, the son of a university professor. This affective detachment helped him pass through the doors of a world where he always felt himself to be an interloper – and to appropriate the alien culture treated with derision by the popular classes. During a lesson on music, discipline of distinction par excellence, when the teacher asked for the identity of the composer of a musical extract, the young Didier Eribon was astounded to hear this boy give the correct answer after only a few bars, and found his certainties wavering. He, who found this lesson grotesque and 'classical music' unbearable – at home, should one happen on a radio programme broadcasting it, it was switched off with the comment: 'we're not at church' – discovered that the

---

50 Ibid., p. 120.

boy he wanted to please listened religiously to a classical piece, could recognize it and appreciate it.[51]

Although the relationship did not last long, fascination with this boy, who adored what he abhorred, stimulated a desire to please him and resemble him. Eribon endeavoured to write like him and, following his example, tended to compromise with the educational order, rather than resisting the established discipline. Eribon emphasizes the determining influence of this friendship, which opened up for him the educated world to which he was hitherto impervious, and which his class habits inclined him to refuse. Thus, this encounter played the role of a social counterweight, helping him to come down on the side of culture rather than passing it by.[52]

The power of desire and the strength of friendship can thus, for a time at any rate, abolish class distance and lead to the embrace of alien models. Like any cultural shock, an amicable or amorous encounter between beings of a different class is accompanied by a recasting of identity, by an opening up to an otherness one wishes to make one's own and become part of. This adventure does not unfold without friction or resistance; the misunderstandings and injuries bound up with ignorance of class codes are not easily dispelled. In this respect, we can wholeheartedly subscribe to Eribon's fine definition of friendship: 'two friends are . . . two incorporated social histories that attempt to coexist'.[53]

The power of friendship that shatters social barriers applies a fortiori to love. Love is certainly often blind, but sometimes it induces people to change their outlook. Stendhal's magnificent pages describing Julien Sorel's encounter with Madame de Rénal attest to this power of amorous desire that fells class

---

51   Eribon, *Returning to Reims*, p. 164.
52   Ibid., pp. 165–6.
53   Ibid., p. 166.

prejudices. Against every expectation, Julien does not discover a haughty, contemptuous bourgeoise but a dazzling young woman who is gentle and considerate; while Madame de Rénal, who fears having to place her children in the hands of a crude little peasant, 'a dirty, ill-tempered priest', sees a handsome, timid young man enter with big black eyes.[54] Gradually, the fears bound up with differences of age and fortune fade before the impact of amorous desire. Constantly on his guard, Julien ends up surrendering for a while: 'The silly idea of being regarded as an inferior lover because of his humble birth vanished as well.'[55] In contact with Madame de Rénal, the son of old Sorel cultivates himself and refines his manners, leaving the world of Verrières behind. For him, non-reproduction takes the form of an amorous education that will nourish his ambitions, giving him the historical and political understanding of the world he lacked when his knowledge was confined to the arcana of theology.[56] However novelistic, this amorous education is not pure fiction. It is inspired by true facts: the encounter between Jean-Jacques Rousseau and Madame de Warens. We can now see why Stendhal's hero regards Rousseau's *Confessions* as 'the one book his imagination drew on to help him picture the world'.[57]

Indeed, the *Confessions* may be regarded as an exemplary autobiography of non-reproduction via an amorous education. Born to a father who was a watchmaker and a mother who died while he was a baby, the young Jean-Jacques was placed in an apprenticeship with an engraver, fleeing at the age of sixteen to become the famous philosopher. In the course of his wanderings, this flight led him to the home of the *curé* of Pontverre, who sent him to the home of a young woman

54 Stendhal, *The Red and the Black*, p. 31.
55 Ibid., p. 95.
56 Ibid., p. 100.
57 Ibid., p. 22.

twelve years his senior, Madame de Warens, who would become his protectress. Just like the future Julien Sorel, Rousseau 'had imagined some sour-faced old zealot'; what he finds is 'a face radiant with grace, blue eyes full of sweetness, a dazzling complexion, the curve of an enchanting bosom'.[58] From the very first start, he feels completely confident and attaches himself to this friendly, cultivated woman, from a superior station in life to his. He becomes her proselyte, living under her direction. Thus, he 'regarded [himself] as the work, the pupil, the friend, the lover, almost, of Madame de Warens'.[59] It was with the person he called 'mama', who initiated him into love, that Rousseau undertook autodidactic studies at Charmettes. He read works of philosophy 'such as the *Logic* of Port-Royal, Locke's *Essay*', and so forth, got on with elementary geometry, and studied Latin laboriously.[60]

The power of love is thus an auxiliary power of transformation in contact with the beloved, and plays the role of a driving force in non-reproduction. Love supplies wings for ascending socially and alleviating guilt about the rupture with the native milieu. But if the social elevator sometimes passes through seventh heaven, we must be wary of clichéd images and avoid concluding that love is the special affect in non-reproduction, or that it serves as an antidote to class struggle. It has specific effects, but is in no way a panacea. If the dream of prince charming or the wealthy beautiful heiress can stimulate the imagination, it hardly generates revolutions, but instead bolsters the social order by imprisoning individuals in the conservatism of expectations.

Besides, non-reproduction is not based on an obligatory affect. A whole particular economy of forces has to be thought

---

58 Jean-Jacques Rousseau, *The Confessions*, transl. Angela Scholar (Oxford: Oxford University Press, 2008), p. 59.

59 Ibid., p. 56.

60 Ibid., p. 231.

in and through each individual trajectory. Consequently, it must be observed that joyous affects do not necessarily play a prominent role. Resentment, hatred, and the rage born of humiliation are just as decisive. This is notably true of Richard Wright. Sullen anger and frustration at not being able to eat his fill, at not having the right to read, at finding himself allotted the role of invisible Negro in life – these will produce an enduring hostility towards whites and entail rejection of the pre-established order. Unlike young blacks, who slavishly comply with the rules, playing the good Negro, jovial and imbecilic in the presence of whites while cordially detesting them and stealing from them behind their backs, he rebels against this degrading role and yearns to attack injustice, to get to grips with it without really knowing how.[61] Like his love of books, anger, fear, and hatred will be driving forces that fuel rebellion against social and racial segregation, lead him to flee without looking back on a miserable condition, and leave the hostile South without remorse in search of a better life: 'and yet out of all the conflicts and the curses, the blows and the anger, the tension and the terror, I had somehow gotten the idea that life could be different, could be lived in a fuller and richer manner'.[62]

In Annie Ernaux, too, the affects are highly ambivalent, for it is not so much love for the rather unlikeable Mademoiselle L. as a form of *amour propre*, or rather a mixture of pride, pain, and silent shame, that induce her to distance herself from the model of her mother and aunts. Pride at being recognized as excellent, and unspeakable shame, the secret pain, of belonging to a milieu that is poor financially and culturally, of living in a family where the code of commercial perfection, which advocates self-control and exemplary behaviour, was smashed to bits the day her father tried to kill her mother. The

---

61 Wright, *Black Boy*, Chapter 10 (pp. 196–209).
62 Ibid., p. 259.

decision to entitle one of her principal auto-socio-biographical books *Shame* leaves no room for doubt in this regard. After that Sunday in June, the author confesses that she 'became unworthy of private education, its standards of excellence and perfection. I began living in shame.'[63]

But this traumatic scene crystallizes a more fundamental shame – social shame – which becomes a way of life inscribed in the body. This is confirmed in *L'Écriture comme un couteau* (Writing as sharp as a knife). Ernaux explains that, through the shame and humiliation experienced during her private school education up to first grade, she discovered the differences between pupils and internalized and lived them – initially in the shape of a personal lack of worth and inferiority, in solitude, without being able to connect them to social origin and clearly understand them as the result of her parents' economic and cultural circumstances.[64] Shame is the confused, painful expression of an awareness of class difference, and gradually becomes a spur to breaking her silence and extricating herself from an intolerable situation.

While the pleasure of succeeding at school, and pride at being distinguished by her educational excellence, facilitated non-reproduction, they were not the preponderant factors. Indeed, in this instance, success is not experienced as a certain victory, but as a kind of anomaly, or fragile opportunity, or incursion into a world that does not belong to you.[65] Profound social and familial suffering were determinants in her career as a writer. At least that is what she confides in connection with *A Man's Place*:

> I think that everything in *A Man's Place* – its form, its voice, its content – was born of pain. The pain that came to me in

---

63 Ernaux, *Shame*, p. 92.
64 Ernaux, *L'Écriture comme un couteau*, p. 69.
65 Ibid.

adolescence when I began to distance myself from my father, a former worker who was now the owner of a small café-grocery. A nameless pain, a mixture of incomprehension and rebellion (why didn't my father read, why did he have 'crude manners', as they say in novels?). Pain one is ashamed of, which one can neither avow nor explain to anyone. And then the other pain, the pain I had of losing him abruptly, when I came to spend a week at my parents', after having realized his dream of upward mobility: I had become a prof, passed over into the other world, the one for which we were 'humble folk', in the language of condescension.[66]

Suffering is generated by the experience of a distance and by critical questioning, which prevent adherence to the surrounding milieu and call it into question. Ernaux views her world with the eyes of others, as if it were external to her, because she has begun to internalize other norms that enable her to make comparisons – norms of social judgement that stigmatize the lack of culture and refinement in 'humble folk'. Hence, shame at her father's inexplicable bad taste, exacerbated by the suffering of daring to unjustly judge her own people, who are not responsible, and of secretly denying them by severing links. Writing is born out of a pain impelling one to put ills into words, in order to survive and salvage oneself and one's own people. In this sense, non-reproduction can result from a form of sublimation and redemption of suffering, from its transformation into a motivating, creative energy.

In these circumstances, the affects that Spinoza characterizes as sad, such as hatred, anger, or shame, which generally reduce the power of acting, are going to have positive effects by combining with joyous affects. They probably even exercise a more decisive influence on non-reproduction than joyous affects. In fact, the vague desire for a different life,

---

66   Ibid., pp. 32–3.

which is presupposed by the orientation towards a different model from those that prevail, can only arise if there is dissatisfaction, even suffering. The person who feels perfectly happy and suited to their milieu does not long to leave it, and is less open to encounters of friendship or love that might upend her world. The individual who is fully integrated into a social or familial order has no reason to sever her links or aspire to an elsewhere. Quite the reverse, she will be inclined to behave as a guardian of the familial or social temple, and to reproduce the dominant values, denouncing any attempt to escape the common lot. The person who dares to infringe the law of the milieu must therefore have powerful motives, for she comes up against a class conservatism with its formidable train of conformism and normalization, which generally take the form of a three-fold diatribe against illusion, treason, and pretention.

A diatribe against illusion, in the first instance: the desire to step out of line is castigated as a chimera, a vain hope – something encapsulated in the famous formula: 'that's not for the likes of us'. The Manichean division of the social world into 'them' and 'us' (where 'them' refers to the bourgeois and 'us' to the workers, or vice versa) defines class boundaries, positing them as insurmountable barriers – insurmountable barriers not only de facto but de jure, for there is something illegitimate about wanting to cross them, which identifies any such endeavour as a form of intrusion or imposture. The desire for upward mobility in the children of proletarians, or for voluntary proletarianization on the part of some sons of the bourgeoisie who chose to share the working-class condition, are denounced as illusions or mystifications. 'Believe me, however hard we try, we'll never be like them'; or 'they aren't like us'. Political activists who have broken with an easy life to work in a factory have thus often paid the price for it. Despite their sincerity, they are prey to incomprehension and suspicion; they are rarely regarded as 'genuine workers', since they can always quit and rediscover the comfort and contacts inherited from their native milieu.

Next, a diatribe against betrayal. More than a rupture, social ascent is a form of perjury. Interpreted as a denial of one's class of origin, it gives rise to grievances and impugning motives, which tend to blame the black sheep. 'You're rejecting us'; 'you've got contempt for us'; 'you're ashamed of us': the defector is accused of being a social traitor and depicted as a haughty renegade.

Finally, a diatribe against pretention. One should 'know one's place', not 'think oneself superior to others', not 'put on airs', and so on. Parvenus are frowned upon; their newfound affluence rhymes with arrogance, and behind the lack of modesty attributed to them is concealed envy, with its procession of calumnies.

Real or imaginary, this collective censure of illusion, treason, and pretention helps to maintain the established order and yield a ranking, such that no being goes beyond it. By dint of its deterrent effects, it is a significant check on upward social mobility. In these conditions, the existence of a desirable alternative model is not enough to trigger an enduring identification. The ambient milieu must also seem constraining, suffocating, destructive even. That is why only powerful motives, such as an irrepressible desire to put an end to intolerable suffering, impart the strength to free oneself from habitus and banish the fear of being taken for a naïf, a Judas, or a popinjay.

This is brought out by a poetic, uncertain, but highly suggestive etymology of the verb to desire. *De-siderare* is to lack a star, to be bereft of something starlike and staggering that dazzles you and lights up the night of your suffering. In this respect, the obscure object of desire is luminous. It involves reaching for the stars and transforming suffering that radiates into a radiant future. Without sanctifying suffering, it must be acknowledged that it has something positive about it, in as much as it impels people to quit a situation of malaise and discomfort, in search of a more tolerable way of life. That is why it is one of the essential causes of non-reproduction. Being in suffering is being on one's way and desiring the elsewhere of a better life.

The Place and Role of Milieu

This motivational suffering is polymorphous, not confined to social shame. It can express a malaise in class, race, sex, gender, family, which prevents integration into the native milieu and encourages new orientations. Such malaise does not necessarily derive from the introjection of external norms that explode established social frameworks. It can arise from internal pressure from the native milieu, which tends to homogenize individuals by compressing differences. Thus, it is sometimes very difficult to determine whether, at the outset, non-reproduction is to be attributed to the individual, who distances herself from her milieu, or to the milieu, which distances the individual. Rejection of the milieu can be construed in two senses: rejection of a milieu by an individual and rejection of an individual by a milieu. Whichever prevails in the causal order – rejecting milieu or rejected milieu – it is necessary to think this twofold dynamic and grasp both its facets, which are mutually reinforcing. Consequently, it is possible to write the same history in two, necessarily correlated ways, conceiving non-reproduction as importation of an alternative model into the existing milieu and as exportation of an individual who does not belong in the existing milieu into a foreign milieu.

The story of Julien Sorel may be understood in line with this dual interpretative grid. If the young Julien has ambition, if he successively identifies with Napoleon, Rousseau – the ecclesiastical models of the abbot and the bishop – and then with the figure of the noble, it is because he does not belong in his familial and social milieu. He is rejected because he does not resemble the other offspring. The elder sons are cast in the image of the father; they have his virile robustness and reproduce his way of life. They are presented as a species of giant, chopping the trunks of fir trees with their heavy axes.[67] By contrast, so fine are Julien's features that he has the appearance of a young girl; and he is distinguished from his brothers not only by a slender physique, unsuitable for heavy labour, but by his intellectual tastes. He likes to read in a milieu where reading is considered a waste of time, a habit for the lazy. Julien therefore appears as a sickly, shy child with his very pale complexion and extremely pensive appearance. He is not part of the robust line of woodcutters and cannot take his place in the social and familial order. He is subject to reprisals or bad treatment in a milieu that cannot stand him, and which he cannot stand. The rejection is mutual. Old Sorel abhors his son, and Julien fully reciprocates his abhorrence: 'The butt of everyone's scorn at home, he hated his brothers and his father.'[68] The father is amazed to discover that Monsieur de Rénal is ready to offer Julien the unhoped-for sum of 300 francs per annum, on top of food, lodging, and clothing; and he seeks to find out how such an eminent man could want to take a good-for-nothing like his son into his home.[69] He seizes on the boon of ridding himself of a 'revolting bookworm', and skilfully negotiates his departure.[70] Thus, it is just as much a case of Julien escaping his milieu as of his milieu expelling him.

In this sense, non-reproduction is simply the continuation of reproduction by other means. The social order is preserved by the expulsion of an element that threatens it, which

---

67 Stendhal, *The Red and the Black*, p. 18.
68 Ibid., p. 20.
69 Ibid., p. 18.
70 Ibid., p. 21.

introduces disorder, as it does not conform to the prevalent model. 'I'm going to be rid of you, and my saw will do all the better for it', says old Sorel to his son by way of farewell.[71] Non-reproduction thus emerges as the ruse of reproduction. Far from contravening it, it helps to maintain it by excluding anything that might destroy it. Anyone not in their place is condemned to be displaced, literally and figuratively. Not to have a place is to be exposed to a migrant future.

The question of place in the family or the class is therefore crucial. It is no accident that Annie Ernaux ended up titling her book *A Man's Place*, after having given it the provisional title of *Elements for a Family Ethnology*.[72] For this notion makes it possible to identify the position everyone occupies in the social and familial space; to assess whether it is sustainable, fixed, or mobile, depending on the ties that bind or distend it. When possible, identification with the dominant model confers a stable basis, and facilitates integration into the familial and social order. But when it is not, on account of a sense of alterity engendered by a more or less vague sense of being apart, one too many, different, or deviant, a breach opens up in reproduction, tempting one to branch out and pursue a singular trajectory, in order to survive and assert oneself. Lack of recognition, being ignored, even contempt from those around one, condemnation, and public banishment – these encourage the 'black sheep' and 'ugly ducklings' to leave. It is hardly surprising if children who are undesired, unloved, or victims of family and social opprobrium are inclined to leave their native milieu to seek a place in the sun and take their revenge on fate.

Thus, Richard Wright discovers that he was always the black sheep of his family, which had feared him since childhood, when he set fire to the curtains and nearly killed

---

71   Ibid.
72   See Ernaux, *L'Écriture comme un couteau*, p. 34.

everyone. When he suddenly re-experiences a scene from his adolescence, in which he kept his Uncle Tom at bay with the threat of his razors, he sees himself for the first time through the eyes of others; and understands that he must have seemed during all those years like a violent boy ready for anything. He realizes the bad reputation that sticks to him and is absolutely appalled. Thus, the abrupt revelation of the precise character of his relations with his family dramatically alters the course of his existence and makes him decide to leave the house and part with his family for good.[73]

In and through the cooperation of different forms of determination, mutually supporting one another, non-reproduction can certainly occur. But how can we fail to see that the way in which the fairies bend over the cradle, and the collective choir chants everyone's deeds and misdeeds, defining a future and delineating a destiny? The choice of a baptismal name gives vent already to a desire; and sometimes the only thing required is a simple first name that does not attach you to anyone, and does not inscribe you in any line of descent, for you to be prompted to part. How can you exist if your parents wish you had not been born, if they give you the role of the dead one, and have you replace a child who died prematurely by even giving you his or her first name? Is not to part to die a little, and indirectly to satisfy the parents' more or less conscious desire? How to remain when one is branded with unworthiness, because one is the child of sin, the despised bastard, or the 'faggot' who should be 'smashed'? A place in the closet is decidedly dark and cramped; and the desire to come out and live in the open can lead to emigration in order to gain recognition.

If Didier Eribon identifies with a different model characterized by culture and the intellectual life, under the impetus of a friendly encounter with a young boy from an

---

73 Wright, *Black Boy*, p. 174.

affluent family, it is also, and above all, because 'someone's homosexuality obliges them to find a way out in order to avoid suffocating'.[74] There is no place in his milieu for a young gay, not even a proper noun to define him. Unnameable at best – 'people like you', says his mother, in her embarrassment at referring to him – it is under the seal of insults and jeers that he discovers what he is. The whole circumambient culture throws his infamy in his face and imprisons him in fear and abjection, affixing to him the stigmatized label of 'faggot': 'I was produced by insult; I am the son of shame.'[75]

The homophobia of his father and the working-class milieu lead the young Eribon to quit Reims and his suburb to pursue studies in Paris and frequent the world of culture and gay social venues. His trajectory is typical of young gays, who escape small provincial towns, the rural and working-class milieu, to go and live in big cities where homosexuality is more tolerated, and who construct an identity for themselves through culture in order to differentiate themselves from virile popular values and discover a world of subjectivation, making it possible to sustain and confer meaning on their 'difference'. To be able to accept oneself, to live with one's head held high, it is necessary to invent oneself by relying on figures of distinction, such as the philosopher, the artist, or the intellectual, which make it possible to differentiate oneself positively from those from whom one differs.[76] Sexual non-reproduction of the dominant model is a decisive factor here – even the origin of social non-reproduction, as Eribon senses: 'A bit earlier in this book, discussing my path through school, I described myself as a miracle case. It could

---

74 Eribon, *Returning to Reims*, p. 192.
75 Ibid., p. 194.
76 Ibid., p. 159. See also Didier Eribon, *Réflexions sur la question gay* (Paris: Flammarion, 2012) and *Une morale du minoritaire* (Paris: Fayard, 2001), where Eribon develops this point.

well be that what made that miracle possible for me was my homosexuality.'[77]

Sexual shame converted into gay pride is the engine of social ascent. In Eribon, shame played a key role in non-reproduction in more respects than one: the sexual shame that leads him to remove himself from a homophobic working-class milieu and the social shame of belonging to a poor family, obscured for a while behind the screen of proudly asserted homosexuality. Thus, one form of shame can conceal another, with gay pride serving as a screen for defining a new identity that conceals any reference to social origins.[78]

Thus, a labour of difference and on difference is at work in non-reproduction. That is why we have to think of the place in the class and apply the principle of distinction within the same in order to understand the emergence of exceptional phenomena. Class homogeneity, based on a community of condition, must not serve to conceal the heterogeneity of situations. It is not a question here of playing the individual off against family or class, and believing that being supernumerary makes people bold, different, enterprising, but of understanding how and why, within a given set-up, an individual places herself, or is placed, at the departure gate. For one does not so much choose to depart as one is selected for departure.

When an individual suffers to the extent of departing, the whole familial and social body also suffers and seeks an escape route through her. That is why non-reproduction is never a merely individual adventure, but an expulsion or

---

77 Eribon, *Returning to Reims*, p. 193.

78 On his return to Reims, Eribon finds himself confronting a question long denied: whether taking his homosexuality as a theoretical framework and explanatory principle for his history, and his break with his family, did not provide a good reason for avoiding thinking that the reason for the distance was probably just as much social shame about his origins and the class barrier. See *Returning to Reims*, pp. 22–3.

propulsion by the milieu. Indeed, it can correspond to a *project* of the milieu as well as a *rejection* by it. The desire for a different life created by encounters and various joyous or sad affects is not necessarily the peculiarity of the individual who breaks with the schema of reproduction. It might be the fruit of a familial or collective aspiration that is expressed in and through it. More or less unwittingly, children are the voice of their parents' frustrated desires, and tend to satisfy their desire for revenge on the poverty, shame, and stigmatization to which they have been subjected. Children become the avengers of the suffering created by being less than nothing by seeking to realize the pious dream wherein the last shall be first, and to accomplish parental wishes for a better life for the next generation.

Thus, parents, who despite themselves reproduce an order that crushes them, are going to strive so that their child does not have the same life as them, at the cost of enormous sacrifices, including the greatest – that is, the loss of the child, who is necessarily going to remove herself from the family bosom. In her desire to be loved and please her family, the child is going to try to comply with these aspirations and be ejected, almost despite herself, from her milieu. Non-reproduction is the singular form that a collective refusal of reproduction can take. In the absence of open rebellion or collective revolution, it is a mute cry of protest by the family which the individual echoes, and which she takes up because it is the place allocated to her in the family. One of the motors of non-reproduction is therefore a yearning for justice, rooted in humiliation and a desire to avenge it, a wish not to repeat the same life generation after generation. Aged twenty-two, Annie Ernaux remarked in her diary that she would write to 'avenge [her] race': to raise her head to erase the insult.

In Didier Eribon, a positive desire to educate himself was nurtured not only by friendship for the young boy he was going to imitate, by sexual and social shame that was to be forgotten through culture, but also by family history, placed under the stamp of infamy and a desire for revenge or rehabilitation; a grandmother who was a teenage single mother, accused of having a liaison with a German officer and having her head shaved at the Liberation, and given a prison sentence for having an abortion; a mother, 'child of sin', who suffered from being a bastard, abandoned by her own mother for several years; a very good female pupil who would have liked to become a primary school teacher, but was unable to pursue her studies because of the war and poverty, who remained extremely bruised and frustrated by the experience.[79] Although he does not concentrate on the family romance, Eribon is conscious of being part of a secretly wounded, humiliated lineage, of inheriting a history where moral shame compounds social misery and profoundly marks his mother's personality and subjectivity. He recognizes that this had to have profound repercussions on his youth and on what was going to happen next.[80] The shame is repeated from one generation to the next, being displaced onto his homosexuality. He therefore has to take emotional responsibility for a past he cannot change, to transform liabilities into assets by winning legitimacy in the world of culture, which also rehabilitates his whole family through him.

Eribon's case is far from exceptional. In the village of T., the pupils who eluded social reproduction under the auspices of their teacher had something in common: a mother, or even two parents, with a strong desire to continue their studies beyond school certificate by virtue of very good results, but who, for want of financial resources, had had to resign themselves to joining the world of work very early on, sometimes from the age of nine, to earn a living for their family. Through the cruelty of fate and birth, one of them had to abandon her

79 Ibid., p. 75.
80 Ibid.

aspirations and become a chamber maid in a hotel, with her meagre wage serving to help finance the studies of her younger sister – the pioneer of non-reproduction in the village. In these circumstances, it is not surprising to find that this sacrificial woman had two children who escaped reproduction. The elder of them, who became a university professor, is the one who secured maximum distance from the social order, in the course of her own life making the transition from the status of primary-school teacher, and then secondary-school teacher, to that of university teacher–researcher and professor, which generally occurs over several generations.

But what is played out in a singular instance of social ascent is the revenge not only of the sacrificed family but sometimes also that of the group, the tribe, or the village in its entirety. In the same village of T., where kinship ties are very close, the inhabitants – poorer than those of the surrounding hamlets on account of the altitude and a mindset more focused on religious faith and spirituality than material goods – are extremely proud of counting 'intellectuals' among their community, and brilliantly distinguishing themselves from their neighbours by this claim to fame, which transforms contempt for them into silent envy. 'The backward ones' thus prove that they are 'brains', and are more than a match for all those who thought they could relegate them to the bottom of the heap. The valorization of local children who have succeeded extends beyond the family and also represents a powerful lever of social ascent. Understanding non-reproduction means thinking a trajectory that is not solitary, but in solidarity with a familial or social milieu that in a way prompts or authorizes it. One does not part all on one's own; one is cast out or sustained by the milieu.

Besides, the sustaining milieu is not necessarily the native one. Social mobility can be encouraged by the dominant class not out of philanthropy, but from a need to train an elite of specialists and supervisors to satisfy its economic and social interest. The best pupils from popular strata then form a pool upon which it is free to draw. Nizan's hero, Antoine Bloyé, son of a worker and a housewife, having become a petty-bourgeois who has stepped out of line, is the perfect example. He is the pure product of the industrial revolution, which in the second half of the nineteenth century required executives and new human resources. It is no accident that, in 1858, parliament passed a law on professional teaching, or that schools of arts and professional schools flourished in these years. First in his division at school, young Antoine is caught up in this movement of fabrication of a petty-bourgeois class in the service of shareholders and bosses:

> Higher destinies are reserved for the sons of the big bourgeoisie, the bourgeoisie of the liberal professions – destinies embellished by the passwords of the humanities. But what tremendous reserves exist among the gifted sons of workers, what an inexhaustible source of faithful subordinates! They are needed; they are enticed with promises of a great future and equal opportunity, the dawn of democracy. Each worker's son has in his satchel the diploma of an overseer of men, the passport of a bourgeois.[81]

Certainly, the transclass does not enter through the front door, but remains, as it were, on the landing, like Antoine, 'who will not sprinkle his speech with bouquets culled from M. Larousse's *Compendium of Latin Words and Phrases* or the *Garden of Greek Roots*'.[82] Nevertheless, with all due respect to Stendhal, the 'upper' class does not always strive to prevent the 'lower' class from rising. It might encourage its rise to a certain degree, based on a calculation of its interests.

---

81 Paul Nizan, *Antoine Bloyé*, transl. Edmund Stevens (New York: Monthly Review, 1973), p. 58.
82 Ibid., pp. 42–3.

But whatever the lever, class starting point or class destination, a problem remains in abeyance: how is it that, within the same family, two children, inheritors of an identical history, raised in similar fashion, with the same sexual orientation, have such different social destinies; that one reproduces the original model while the other departs radically from it? How do we explain the uniqueness of trajectories and the divergence of paths, when the starting conditions are seemingly similar?

This is a problem tackled by John Edgar Wideman in *Brothers and Keepers*, translated into French as *Am I My Brother's Keeper?* Wideman was born in the black ghetto of Pittsburgh in Pennsylvania, and experienced a radically different social fate from that of his brother, Robby. Despite the poverty and racism, he became an academic, and then a recognized writer, not only in the black community but outside it, whereas his brother Robby ended up being imprisoned for life following a murder. *Brothers and Keepers* is presented as a narrative in two voices, the point being to understand the sequence of causes and circumstances that led two fellow beings, two brothers, to experience such a different fate. Although John Edgar is the author, the book arose out of meetings with his brother in the visiting room, and relates the story of their two lives concurrently.

At the start, the difference in respective destinies is presented as a fortuitous accident. Robby's history boils down to a simple, familiar pattern that turned out badly: the armed robbery of a fence in the company of two villains, Michael Dukes and Cecil Rice. But a man gets killed because he made a move, and one of the accomplices, thinking he was hiding a pistol under his jacket, panicked, and fired.[83] There was a high price to pay for this tragic mistake: the death of a young man and three lives

---

83 John Edgar Wideman, *Brothers and Keepers* (Edinburgh: Canongate, 2018), p. 11.

shattered by life imprisonment. Initially, Wideman foregrounds the similarity and interchangeability of the places, and accounts for the difference by recourse to contingent external factors such as bad luck or an arbitrary sentence. He regards the imprisonment of his brother, his flesh and blood, raised by the same parents in the same house, as a form of malfunctioning of the system, because any other reason would be far too compromising. He interprets this judicial error as a sign of his own vulnerability, because he could be in his place behind bars.[84] In opting for a logic of class identity, racial identity, and the interchangeability of places, Wideman prevents himself from understanding the differences other than as a twist of fate, the result of good or bad luck, and thus transforms destinations into destinies. In short, the difference remains a mystery because the invocation of fortune, brandished like a *deus ex machina*, obscures the causal determinants at work, serving as a mask for ignorance.

In a second phase, Wideman discovers that identification with his brother – which is a way of exonerating him, of exonerating himself through him, and of distinguishing himself from criminals with the help of statements like 'You're not like these others. You're my brother, you're like me. Different' – is a form of negation of each person's uniqueness.[85] The first moment, which consists in saying 'you're like me', is certainly necessary, for it represents an act of recognition of kinship and similarity. But it must not obscure difference. My brother is not another me; he is other than me. Wideman gradually comes to realize that he must see his brother as he is, with his own history and references, and understand his difference, over and above resemblance, by quitting the habit of listening to himself listening to him.[86]

---

84   Ibid., p. 68.
85   Ibid.
86   Ibid., p. 107.

The work of understanding is therefore not confined to establishing a community of sympathy with the other, but involves affirming an irreducible singularity. The divergence of paths then emerges as the result of a twofold dynamic: the causality of difference and the causality of the world that shapes and transforms it by assigning a place to each person. That, at least, is the observation made by Wideman: 'The world had seized on the difference, allowed me room to thrive, while he'd been forced into a cage. Why did it work out that way? What was the nature of the difference?'[87] He thus moves from chance to necessity by abandoning the idea of a 'lottery' in favour of the idea of the efficacy of difference under the combined impact of the external world.

The whole point is to determine the nature of this difference. The inquiry does not lead to research of an essentialist kind, consisting in identifying pre-established unique beings. In fact, the difference between the two brothers is not so much an ontological difference as a topological one, if we may put it like that. It is rooted chiefly in the place of each person in the sibling group. John is the eldest and carries the family's hopes for a better life for the next generation. He is inspired by the idea, commonplace in the ghetto, that it is necessary to rise socially and wash away the insult to blacks, 'to get ahead, to make something of myself' by getting to college.[88] He has escaped poverty and negritude in order to join the white world, the sole genuine guarantor of his success. His trajectory follows the mandatory stages of the social success of the young American black from a poor district: the educational stage, 'good grades' and 'good English', which widen the gap and initiate the departure; the economic stage, 'a scholarship and a train ticket over the mountains to Philadelphia'; finally, the geographical stage – exile – which merges displacement

---

87 Ibid.
88 Ibid., p. 37.

and *déclassement*, with rare returns to the cradle experienced as signs of confirmation of superiority and success.[89]

By contrast, Robby's trajectory is characterized by his place as younger brother in the sibling group. He is the youngest of the family, and his problem is to affirm himself in his unique-ness, as John was able to, without following paths already marked out by his brothers. Robby wants to be someone, not the little last one who people predict will be good at school, like all the Widemans, mapping out the road to follow. At school or in sport, he cannot do anything his brothers and sister have not already done, and he refuses to imitate them, as he confides to John Edgar: 'something inside me said no. Didn't want to be like the rest of yous. Me, I had to be a rebel.'[90]

The parting of the ways derives not from an innate differ-ence but a differentiation, which occurs historically in interac-tion with the surrounding milieu and the family set-up. The model of the rebel, who defies the law and introduces a reign of terror, impresses itself on Robby in his bid to find a place for himself, 'to be a star', 'to make it big'.[91] The culture of the rebel posture is presented as a protest against both the milieu of poverty and the traditional solutions offered to young blacks from the ghettos: salvation through sport or school. The places of the sportsman and the intellectual being occu-pied by his brothers, Robby has to discover new territory and follow in no one's tracks.

His career is subject to a twofold dynamic of distinction that takes non-reproduction to its paroxysm. Robby refuses to reproduce his parents' life, but rejects the non-reproduction of his elders. He regards salvation through sport or school as a form of class treason, *embourgeoisement*, and conformism. For

---

89 Ibid.
90 Ibid., p. 119.
91 Ibid.

these kinds of non-reproduction are authorized and encouraged by society, insofar as they confirm the established order without ever challenging it. Non-reproduction thus appears as a safety valve for reproduction, as the most subtle form of submission. Conversely, the rebel posture embraced by Robby is intended as a radical, original figure of non-reproduction: 'I wanted the glamour. I wanted to sit high up. Figured out school and sports wasn't the way. I got to thinking my brothers and sister was squares. Loved youall but wasn't no room left for me. Had to figure out a new territory. I had to be a rebel.'[92] Wishing to make a place in the sun for himself, Robby will find himself back 'in the dark'. That is how he shines and makes a name for himself.

It is of little moment here that the model of the rebel is just as conventional as that of the sportsperson or intellectual, and that transgression does not overturn the social order, which penalizes it by marginalization or imprisonment. Self-assertion leads to self-differentiation against a background of identity and a denial of interchangeability, so that the ultimate form of difference consists in not reproducing the dominant model of non-reproduction.

Ingenium or Complexion

In the final analysis, to understand the assertion of a unique trajectory at work in non-reproduction, we must not confine ourselves to grasping 'what each person makes of what has been made of them', as Sartre invites us to. Instead, we must analyse what they make of what has been made of them *and* of others. The terms of the problem do not boil down to a face-off between a unique being and their milieu in some atomistic, individualistic logic. They involve appreciating the

---

92 Ibid.

complex ways in which everyone carves out a place in being, defining themselves by identification and differentiation in a given space with and against others. Non-reproduction obeys a schema of interconnection wherein the individual cannot be conceived as an isolated being who secedes from her own class. If she appears to be an exception, she is not an island cut off from the rest, an empire in an empire, to speak like Spinoza. Exceptions only exist in an environment that makes them possible, so that an atypical trajectory does not represent a deviation. It happens with the cooperation of the milieu, at the intersection of its impulses and repulsions. It is the fruit not of some disruption but of a combination of rules different from those that generally obtain. The transclass is not so much a solitary hero as a herald conveying personal and collective aspirations, whether of the family, the village, the neighbour-hood, race or class, sex, or gender.

Non-reproduction is therefore not an individual phenome-non but trans-individual. It cannot be understood if the economic, sociological, familial, and affective forms of deter-mination at work in each person's history are conceived sepa-rately. It involves thinking the primacy neither of personal volition nor of social and material conditions, as if desire was not determined by economics and sociology, and economics and sociology were not in return shot through with affects. As Annie Ernaux rightly points out, 'the private is also and always something social, because a pure self where others, laws, history are not present is inconceivable'.[93] Reciprocally, reluc-tance to take account of the existence of affects, which some-times translates into a contemptuous rejection of 'psycholo-gism', or an a priori distrust of psychoanalysis in general (as if there were only one form of it), prevents an understanding of how the emotions shape the social body.

Non-reproduction invites us to think imbricated histories

---

93   Ernaux, *L'Écriture comme un couteau*, p. 152.

and intertwined causes. It is the product not of *a* first determinant cause that could be presented as *the* cause but of a singular arrangement of multiple causes whose outcome is a trajectory. In this respect, no one cause on its own is decisive. Neither ambition, nor the presence of alternative familial or educational models, nor the existence of financial incentives and favourable socioeconomic measures can explain it on their own. Nor is there some special affect, such as shame, the desire for justice or recognition, that can be brandished as primordial cause. The affects are marked by ambivalence, and can incline human beings in opposite directions, depending on their own intensity and the forces with which they combine or clash. Didier Eribon thus notes the fundamental ambivalence of shame, which by turns generates fear or daring, and which can as easily impel people to maintain their silence as to break it, to submit to the established order as rebel against it.[94] In this respect, any isolated determinant can be at most a necessary, but insufficient, condition of the emergence of transclasses. That is why non-reproduction mobilizes a combinatory form of thinking, of cooperation or connection, and requires analysis of a causal network or cluster.

This raises the question of how to subsume the set of affective, economic, political, and historical forms of determination conducive to the emergence of transclasses under the unity of a concept. It is clear that non-reproduction cannot be based on class habitus that produce the opposite effect. It does not involve their abolition or a complete break with the native milieu, but it does presuppose a new arrangement of forms of determination. In this respect, it brings into play not so much *genius* as *engineering* – it appeals not to a natural disposition to create something original, but to a complex apparatus synthesizing the determinants constitutive of an individual in

94 Didier Eribon, *Retour sur Retour à Reims* (Paris: Cartouche, 2011), p. 44.

conjunction with their surrounding milieu. We should therefore think the *ingenium* of the transclass rather than the
genius, understood as an exceptional capacity for invention.

The two terms, derived from the same verb – *genere* – which
means to produce, to create, were not originally opposed. In
philosophical language, from Latin antiquity to the modern
age, *ingenium* is a concept that refers to the mind, its intelligence or skill, expressing its native capacity to produce ideas
and works, its theoretical and practical inventiveness.[95] But
its meaning was to shift from the innate to the acquired. In his
Totius latinatis lexicon of 1865, Forcellini identified four
interconnected meanings of the word. In a broad sense, *ingenium* refers to the innate qualities of a thing. In a narrow
sense, it applies to human beings and encompasses the set of
their natural dispositions, character traits, and mores, and
more especially designates their intelligence and capacity for
invention. Finally, it serves to characterize the human beings
endowed with these faculties.[96] Although the term has no
exact equivalent in French, it is from the last meaning that the
noun *ingéniosité* (ingenuity) and the adjective *ingénieux*
(ingenious) derive.

But what concerns us here is not the reference to innate
natural dispositions, but the inflection which, within the same
filiation, the idea of *ingenium* introduces into that of *genius*.
Emphasizing human mores and manners, it highlights the
historical dimension of the nature of a being and its fashioning by external causes, such that its distinctive singularity is
not so much constitutive as constituted. If inventiveness and
originality exist, they are the fruits not so much of native
dispositions as of capacities that develop depending on
circumstances.

---

95 On this point, see Alain Pons, 'Ingenium', *Sententiae* 22: 1
(2010), pp. 183–9.
96 Ibid., p. 183.

This is the sense in which the concept of *ingenium* is used, for example, in Spinoza's philosophy. *Ingenium* refers to the set of an individual's singular characteristic traits, which are the product of shared history, her own habits, and her encounters with the world. *Ingenium* might be defined as a complex of sedimented affects constitutive of an individual, her way of life, her judgements and behaviour. It is rooted in the dispositions of the body, and comprises physical and mental ways of being alike. It is constituted out of the traces imprinted in us by things, which the body retains – traces out of which we form images, representations, or which we reconfigure, interpreting them as signs, combining them in accordance with the logic peculiar to our mind and its previous experience of thinking. The concept expresses the recognizable individuality of a human being as well as a people.

Thus, Spinoza refers to the *ingenium* of the man living under the guidance of reason, who is differentiated from the ignorant person; of the *ingenium* of the Jewish people, tough and rebellious, as it has been shaped by its religious and political history.[97] It is clear in this context that *ingenium* does not refer to an innate natural disposition. Spinoza refuses to attribute the Jewish people's rebellious *ingenium* to a nature, but attributes it to their laws and customs.[98] *Ingenium* has something irreducibly singular about it, and is not readily transposable from one individual to another. This is one of the reasons why Spinoza asserts that 'no one is obliged by the law of nature to live according to the views [*ingenium*] of another person' – although everyone tyrannically aspires to get others to live according to theirs.[99] *Ingenium* makes it possible to think the diversity of individuals without invoking a common

---

97 Spinoza, *Ethics*, p. 151; Benedict de Spinoza, *Theological-Political Treatise*, ed. Jonathan Israel, transl. Jonathan Israel and Michael Silverthorne (Cambridge: Cambridge University Press, 2016), p. 74.

98 Ibid., p. 224.

99 Ibid., p. 11.

nature or an immutable individual nature. Spinoza stress the diversity of *ingenium*, which lies behind the indefinite variety of judgements and beliefs, particularly in the preface to the *Theological-Political Treatise*: 'human beings have very different minds [*ingenium*], and find themselves comfortable with very different beliefs; what moves one person to devotion provokes another to laughter'.[100]

While the term *ingenium* is sometimes rendered in French by *esprit* or *tempérament* or *caractère*, the word *complexion* probably renders it best in a Spinozist context. It clearly conveys the idea of a complex, singular assemblage of inter-linked physical and mental forms of determination. Appearing in the French language in the thirteenth century, the word refers both to a unique physical constitution (thus one speaks of a fine or coarse complexion) and to particular inclinations or forms of behaviour. For example, Montaigne evokes the solitary, melancholic complexion that impels people to engage in the study of books.[101]

Historically, the concept refers in the first instance to determinations of a physical and physiological kind, such as colour, skin complexion, or its texture. It concerns not only physical appearance and the external aspect of the body but its organic dispositions. Complexion is thus a medical term that designates the physical constitution of a person considered from the standpoint of their health. This constitution is viewed in its uniqueness, with its particularities and variants, and it brings together natural, biological, and other characteristics resulting from the vicissitudes of an individual's personal history. From a medical angle, complexion is defined as an assemblage of interacting physical determinations.

---

100   Ibid., p. 10.
101   Michel de Montaigne, *Essays*, Book I, Chapter 26 in *The Complete Works*, transl. Donald M. Frame (London: Everyman's Library, 2003).

The term *complexion* was next used in philosophy to characterize the organization of an individual's physical and mental dispositions – their inclinations, tendencies, or moods. The word, which comes from the Latin *complexio*, coined from the prefix *con* (with) and the root *plexus*, derived from the past participle of *plectere* (to tie, to twine), clearly expresses the complex intertwining of the threads that compose the fabric of an existence and attach it to that of others.

Construed thus, *ingenium* or complexion refers to the chain of determinations woven together to form the weft of a unique life. They preserve the idea of originality from the notion of genius, but strip it of any innate, transcendent dimension, foregrounding the historical product of an industrious weaving mill in conjunction with a milieu. They thus invite us to think the transclass as a being caught up in a tangle of relations and affects that are combined and composed to yield a new configuration. Even so, this does not involve saying with Montaigne that 'like puppets we are moved by outside strings'.[102] Like any human being, the transclass is not made of wood and, although she does not pull all the strings, she also weaves the web of her existence, striving to unpick its threads, to unknot them, or braid them differently, without ever totally breaking the bond with others, even when she wishes to separate from them. In short, only by thinking in terms of complexion can we explain non-reproduction.

---

102   Ibid., p. 291.

Part II
The Complexion of Transclasses

The difficulty is not to rise, but in rising to remain one's self.

Jules Michelet, *The People*

Spinning the textile metaphor, the complexion of transclasses emerges as a contexture, a unique way in which the parts of an existence, taken as a whole, are linked and organized. It is less the expression of a form than of a formation, where new stitches are added to the initial tapestry. But if the complexion of the transclass is defined as the union of physical and mental characteristics intertwined under the impact of a plural causality, the nature of this interlacing remains to be understood. From union to unity is a long way. A knot can be more or less loose, and bonds more or less tight, so that the contexture is not necessarily robust and enduring. Early on, Montaigne shared his scepticism about the idea of a constant human nature: 'it has often seemed to me that even good authors are wrong to insist on fashioning a consistent and solid fabric [*contexture*] out of us'.[1] And he adds: 'we change like that animal which takes the color of the place you set it on'.[2] What, a fortiori, are we to say of the transclass? Is she a chameleon lacking in all consistency? A being of bric-a-brac? A being in transit? The issue is what is woven behind the composite tangle of forms of determination.

Here it is interesting to note that when, in 1880, Littré's *Dictionary of the French Language* equated complexion in the

---

1   Michel de Montaigne, *The Complete Essays of Montaigne*, transl. Donald M. Frame (London: Everyman's Library, 2003), p. 290.

2   Ibid., p. 291.

philosophical sense with an interweaving, or a union, it referred to the text of the Sixth Meditation, where Descartes defined the nature of man in the broad sense as 'the complex [*complexion*] of all that God has given me'.[3] Taken in this sense, complexion comprises the set of data pertaining to the mind, to the body, and also those that bring into play their union. The concept of complexion makes it possible to pull together under the unity of a single nature the assemblage of physical, mental, and psychophysical determinations. Such unity is not self-evident. The union of the soul and the body is a fact that remains unintelligible in Descartes, for it brings together two substances that are different in kind: 'extension' and 'thinking'. The united soul and body do not change nature and do not form a third substance. The formation of a third substance is impossible, because its existence would have to be conceived on the basis of thinking substance and extended substance. This third substance therefore cannot exist: without the cooperation of God, a created substance, by definition, has no need of another created substance to exist. Consequently, substances do not fuse, so that their union does not abolish the distinction, and dualism persists.

The rare use of the term *complexion* therefore enables Descartes to regard man as a unified totality, and to get around the metaphysical difficulty bound up with the possibility of a conjunction of two distinct substances. When he speaks of nature as complexion, the French philosopher refers to the nub of the union, dispensing with reference to the concept of substance. But, in thus avoiding speaking of the soul and the body as substances, he runs the risk of de-substantializing them and, despite himself, paving the way for a conception of

---

3 René Descartes, *Meditations on First Philosophy*, 'Sixth Meditation', in *Philosophical Writings*, ed. and transl. Elizabeth Anscombe and Peter Thomas Geach (London: Nelson's University Paperbacks, 1975), p. 116.

complexion as an accidental assemblage of multiple elements. Henricus Regius will not fail to rush into this breach by identifying man as a being by accident, and will start a polemic on the subject of his ontological status.

Looking beyond Descartes, the concept of complexion implies that there is nothing substantive about the nature of transclasses, since it is very difficult to envisage the existence of a subject or substratum that remains invariant in and through change. The transclass experiences a double life whose unity is, to say the least, problematic, since change is sometimes of such a kind that we may doubt whether the same human being is involved. Her existence is placed under the seal of mutation and mobility.

This is clearly expressed by the term *complexion*, whose great semantic richness we must underscore. In the seventeenth century, complexion designates both fantasy and caprice, and refers to the changing character of a being. The 1694 dictionary of the Académie Française illustrates this meaning with a piquant example (for a change): 'This woman got used to all the complexions of her husband.'[4] In her turn, the transclass is a creation with many faces, who has had to adapt, and who asks people to adapt to her so as to decipher the mobile features of her personality. She is a being of metamorphosis, so that we can ask not only what survives of her former self, but also whether the idea of a self-identical I defying the changes becomes irrelevant.

1 Disidentification

Non-reproduction highlights the limits of the idea of identity and the classification of individuals in social categories, which

---

4 *Dictionnaire de l'Académie françoise*, 1st edn, 2 vols (Paris: Coignard, 1694).

do not enable us to make complete sense of the trajectories of transclasses in their singularity. To think their complexion, we must therefore take our distance from the classical conceptual apparatus and critique it. Identity, whether personal or social, assumes the existence of individuals who remain the same and who are reducible to a certain number of persistent features in spite of change. Whatever the definition of it, it always involves recognition of a substratum that persists throughout all alterations. Whether this substratum is conceived in the form of a substantive self, the person, the subject, and so on, it is invariably presented as an immutable kernel withstanding change. The tendency to seek to define individuals by constant characteristics that differentiate them from others thus leads to the development of principles of identification such as categorization in terms of gender, sex, race, or class.

But transclasses demonstrate that it is not certain that human beings possess an identity like a visiting card, making it possible to recognize them or confer a status on them. We have to accept that individuals who do not reproduce necessarily have a floating or fluctuating identity, because they are not assignable to their native milieu and are demarcated from their peers. Change and mutation rule their existence. They are therefore characterized by a process of disidentification, decoupling, which frees them from their family and their class.

Such disidentification is not reducible to the temporary stage in which they conquer a novel identity, for ultimately, they are not assimilable to their new milieu. They unfailingly bear the traces of the native milieu, if only those of past history, so that they will never have the same shared heritage as those whose condition they are going to share. Transclasses thus call into question the static principles of the division of individuals into clearly defined social categories and the postulate of a fixed identity, because it is very hard to assign them properties or qualities that lead to their being recognized as belonging to this or that class.

That is why the concept of recognition used in the field of ethics and politics is problematic in its turn when it presupposes a negated identity that is to be triumphantly asserted. In most cases, the struggle for recognition is based on aiming to secure acceptance for a sexual, social, or racial identity, voluntarily or by force, and to compel respect in order to be accorded dignity and specific rights. In so doing, it always runs the risk of imprisoning the individual in fixed, abstract determinations, which, by definition, are recognizable: Woman, Homosexual, Worker, Bourgeois, Boss, and so on. Politically, it is certainly legitimate to muster under the banner of the concept of identity, because in order to mobilize individuals effectively in a struggle for their rights, it is necessary to emphasize the shared features that unite them and define their condition.

Philosophically, problematics of recognition are deficient when they suggest that individuals boil down to a fixed identity and reduce them to a genus or a universal common notion that does not express their singular essence. When the struggle for recognition fails, the identities affixed to individuals emerge as the supreme form of alienation, since they are locked in perpetuity into immutable characteristics – their sex, their race, their social status. By contrast, the concept of complexion prompts us to take on board subtle differences, the particularity of beings, and to think conflictual relations in terms of cognition rather than recognition. A cognitive process seems more appropriate, for what is at stake is understanding a reality that escapes from itself and does not come to a halt at a shared characteristic. That is why thinking in terms of complexion involves a break with identity thinking and encourages a deconstruction of the personal and social self.

The Deconstruction of the Personal Self

In this respect, the transclass emerges as an exemplary figure of the de-substantialization of the self. She radicalizes the experience of the inconsistency of the self, and the inconstancy of its qualities, to which Pascal invites us in the *Pensées*. In the famous fragment 688/323, which opens with the question 'What is the self?', Pascal reveals the nullity of our being and of everyone's vain claim to be loved for their person. This self, which we make the centre of everything and believe to be everywhere, is not to be found anywhere. Pascal dissolves it in three phases wherein, blinded by self-love, the putative self is experienced as an illusion under the gaze of others and the feelings they bring to it. First of all, he encourages each and every one of us to decentre ourselves and adopt the perspective of a spectator at their window: 'A man goes to the window to see the people passing by; if I pass by, can I say he went there to see me? No, for he is not thinking of me in particular.'[5] Under the indifferent gaze of others, no one emerges from the anonymity of the passer-by. I am not *a* person, I am *no* one. Far from being a substantive self, I pass for a passer-by. This experiment in self-dissolution applies perfectly to the transclass, who is the passer-by par excellence. By definition, she is a being of passage, a passing being, who leaves her milieu, is going to walk away from it while often remaining an alien in her new sphere.

Next, Pascal varies the viewpoint by considering the self not with the detached eye of the onlooker, but with a lover's gaze. He narrows the angle of the window by limiting it to the I–you relationship, which breaks with the impersonality of the 'them' or 'they' and the parading crowd. It might be thought that love makes all the difference in the world. In

---

5   Blaise Pascal, *Pensées*, transl. A. J. Kraisheimer (Harmondsworth: Penguin, 1983), 688/323, p. 245.

distinguishing the fortunate, chosen one, it abolishes non-differentiation and frees it from passing being, from mortal becoming, by promising eternal being. In preferring me to any other, does not the one who loves me restore me to the central throne of the unique, substantive self? But what exactly does the person who loves love? Pascal reviews lovable qualities – in the first instance, the physical appearance of the beloved: 'what about a person who loves someone for the sake of her beauty; does he love *her*? No, for smallpox, which will destroy beauty without destroying the person, will put an end to his love for her.'[6] It is clear that, when I am loved for my physical aspect, one loves me for the beauty *in* me, but not *me*. The experience of the passer-by is repeated here in the form of what passes – ephemeral beauty – and the being one tires of, returning her to the indifference of nothingness.

But the illusion of the self is stubborn, and is nourished by the idea that, while physical beauty dies, moral beauty persists. Pascal then delivers the knockout blow: 'And if someone loves me for my judgement or my memory, do they love me? *me*, myself? No, for I could lose these qualities without losing my self.'[7] The mind too can be corrupted, and there is nothing substantive about its qualities, for they are just as perishable as beauty. Old age, accident, illness – and there is an end of the fine mind! Love is therefore not addressed to me, but to qualities given to me. When they perish, love must die. Regardless of whether they are corporeal or spiritual, they are always borrowed qualities; they are not mine, are not me. Pascal may well conclude: 'Where then is this self, if it is neither in the body nor the soul? And how can one love the body or the soul except for the sake of such qualities, which are not what makes up the self, since they

---

6   Ibid.
7   Ibid.

85

are perishable? . . . Therefore we never love anyone, but only qualities.'[8] The self is elusive; it is literally groundless. Stripped of its accidental qualities, it is emptied of its substance and is unworthy to be loved, for it has *nothing* lovable about it. No doubt, Pascal's intention was not to establish that man is irrevocably inconsistent, for he can always discover his substance in Jesus Christ by hating the self and loving God.[9] Even so, the author of the *Pensées* draws attention to the common anthropological condition that the transclass is more aware of than anyone else, since she directly experiences this spectral self by virtue of considerable physical and mental changes.

The story of Martin Eden, an uncouth, uneducated sailor who becomes a writer enamoured of arts and letters, affords a perfect illustration. Jack London's hero changes body and mind to become the opposite of what he was. At ease in the robust body of a belligerent sailor, which makes him successful with women, he becomes ungainly, tangled up in his physique like an elephant in a china shop, when he goes into bourgeois salons. His uncultivated mind and crude language give way to a refined culture and language. Far from heralding the glorious birth of a new self, however, this metamorphosis dissolves and destroys him, to the extent that he feels ghostlike and will soon join the kingdom of shadows by committing suicide. The narrative of a social adventure that goes wrong leaves no doubt on this score:

> He glanced about him at the well-bred, well-dressed men and women, and breathed into his lungs the atmosphere of culture and refinement, and at the same time the ghost of his early youth, in stiff-rim and square-cut, with swagger and toughness, stalked across the room. This figure, of the corner

---

8 Ibid.
9 See ibid., pp. 136–7 (373–476), 148 (417–548).

hoodlum, he saw merge into himself, sitting and talking with
an actual university professor.[10]

But Martin Eden the brilliant writer, timid and paralyzed by
the fear of damaging the furniture with an untoward movement of his shoulder,[11] is just as ghostlike as the sailor of his
youth, 'with a certain swagger to the shoulders and ... the
ideal of being as tough as the police permitted', and whose
'opinions, like [his] clothes, were ready made'.[12] Having
become the darling of socialites and magazines that elicit the
very texts they disdained some years earlier, publishing them
at a high price, Martin Eden has the unhappy consciousness of
being a personality rather than a person, and discovers his
own nothingness. The grilling that occurs in front of his
mirror, at the very start of his social ascent – 'Who are you,
Martin Eden? ... Who are you? What are you? Where do you
belong?' – finally results in a definitive response:

> He drove along the path of relentless logic to the conclusion
> that he was nobody, nothing. Mart Eden, the hoodlum, and
> Mart Eden, the sailor, had been real, had been he; but Martin
> Eden! the famous writer, did not exist. Martin Eden, the
> famous writer, was a vapor that had arisen in the mob-mind
> and by the mob-mind had been thrust into the corporeal being
> of Mart Eden, the hoodlum and sailor.[13]

In this largely autobiographical novel, Jack London is ultimately more Pascalian than Pascal. He shows not only that
the experience of love has nothing to do with the recognition
of a substantive identity, since this emotion is addressed to

---

10 Jack London, *Martin Eden* (New York: Macmillan, 1912), pp.
238–9.
11 Ibid., p. 235.
12 Ibid., pp. 235, 238, 263.
13 Ibid., pp. 104, 386.

qualities which could just as easily not be in me and not be mine, but also that the qualities imputed to me are no such thing. They are pure fictions and projections by others, who begin to savour what they had scorned out of sheepishness, and because it happens to be fashionable. 'I had already written everything before and nobody wanted me then' – such is the leitmotif of a deflated Martin Eden, rejecting the advances of Ruth, the young girl from a good family who finds him lovable now, but who had previously spurned him.[14] Thus, even a loan is a fool's bargain, because people lend me what does not exist, what they do not have. One attempts to mend a tear, as it were, with bright white thread.

Ultimately, we cannot credit the self because everything is borrowed. People affect to ignore this (Pascal tells us) by mistakenly 'scoffing at those who win honour through their appointments and offices, for we never love anyone except for borrowed qualities'.[15] The vain, who seem to confuse being with having, interiority with exteriority, seeking to get themselves admired not for themselves, but for their prestigious positions and top jobs, reveal the truth of the human condition, ready and primed. The malicious smile about them is nothing but the obverse of self-blindness. Thus, people make fun of the parvenu who apes the bourgeois, in the belief that they are encountering a ridiculous caricature of a natural model. Our behaviour and our identities are, however, themselves artificial, and wear out like rags. So, there is nothing surprising about the transclass borrowing an appearance, since, like everyone else, she takes on borrowed qualities. She does not feel comfortable in her clothes, unlike the classy types who mistakenly think they are natural because they have forgotten that custom creates costumes. Pascal's demystification thus takes the form of

---

14 Ibid., p. 390.
15 Pascal, *Pensées*, 688/323, p. 245.

equating intrinsic qualities with extrinsic qualities bound up with rank and social role.

The Deconstruction of the Social Self

Any identity, be it personal or social, is always a form of usurpation in which one takes on qualities that are not de jure qualities. This is what Pascal demonstrates magisterially in the *First Discourse on the Condition of Grandees*, where he addresses a duke to enlighten him on his condition as a rich and powerful great lord, and to reveal to him the exact nature of his condition, with the help of an arresting image. The duke's condition is similar to that of a man cast onto an island because of a storm, who agrees to pass himself off as the king when the inhabitants mistakenly believe they recognize their lost sovereign because of a physical resemblance.[16] Exploiting his good luck, he knows the kingdom does not belong to him and is motivated by two lines of thought, one open where he acts as monarch, and the other hidden where he recognizes his true state and the role of chance in putting him where he is. Equipped with this analogy, Pascal draws the lesson in his apostrophe to the duke:

> Do not imagine that it is by any lesser chance that you possess
> the wealth of which you are master than that by which this

---

16 'To enter into genuine knowledge of your condition, consider it in this image. A man is cast by a storm onto an unknown island, whose inhabitants were at a loss to find their king who had gone missing. And greatly resembling the king in body and face, he is taken for him and recognized as such by the whole population. Initially, he does not know what part to play. But he finally decides to give himself over to his good fortune. He receives all the respect the people wish to pay him and allows himself to be treated as king.' Blaise Pascal, 'Premier discours sur la condition des Grands', in *Oeuvres complètes*, ed. L. Lafuma (Paris: Éditions du Seuil, 1963), p. 366.

man found himself king. You have no right to it of yourself and by your nature, any more than him; and not only the fact that you are the son of a duke, but the fact that you find your-self in the world at all, is the result of an infinite number of contingencies.[17]

The condition of lord is not some natural grandeur, but an established grandeur based exclusively on the will or caprice of legislators. Thus, Pascal continues,

The title whereby you possess your property is not a natural title but one of human establishment. A different turn of imagi-nation in those who made the laws would have made you poor. Only the confluence of chance brought you into the world, with the caprice of laws favourable to you, puts you in posses-sion of all these goods.[18]

One should therefore not confuse a possessor with a legiti-mate owner and, like the shipwrecked man who became king, follow two lines of thought: externally, maintain his rank above the people and, internally, know that he is equal to mere mortals and that he has neither merit nor quality justifying his social position.

This speech can be extended from grandees to transclasses and the human condition as a whole. Like the man fortui-tously cast by storm onto the unknown island, we are cast into the world by chance encounters. Others take us for someone and project onto us a social identity by virtue of appearances, just as the island's inhabitants will take for their king this shipwrecked man who resembles him and recognize him as such. However, he knows he is not king, even if he agrees to wear the robes. Thus, we get ourselves taken for what we are

---

17 Ibid.
18 Ibid.

not. All our postures are impostures and our identities so much role-playing by which we must not be fooled, if we are to avoid misunderstanding ourselves and confounding being and status.

The illusion consists in believing that one is either king of the world or its dregs. Roles and ranks are distributed at the whim of human beings, their caprices and power relations. People treat me as a worker or as a prince. But I am neither the one nor the other; and all violence possibly derives from the fact that an extrinsic determination is erected into an intrinsic essence, endowed with unequal values and rights: 'Your soul and your body,' Pascal says, 'are indifferent to the status of boatman or that of Duke, and there is no natural bond attaching them to one condition rather than another.'[19]

This indifference must not be misinterpreted. Pascal does not mean that all conditions are equivalent, and that everyone should be content with what they are or what they have, because precisely for him everyone is nothing and has nothing. Far from advancing an odious moralizing argument, he intends to emphasize the plasticity of the body and the mind, which can interchangeably lend themselves to one state or another. If some conditions are preferable or easier to endure than others, they are not congenital, and human beings can invariably pass from one to the other.

The concept of complexion therefore offers an alternative to the obsolete idea of self as substance or self as subject, principle of unity and identity of individuals. For it makes it possible to think the plaiting of forms of determination in conjunction with environmental starting-points and destinations. The fact that many individuals fix themselves, or are fixed, under a label or in given circumstances, like chameleons prevented from moving, must not lead us to forget that human life can assume the colours of places where it is spent and that it is

---

19 Ibid.

inscribed in the register of variation and variety. In these circumstances, what differentiates the transclass from her peers is not so much the absence of a substantive self or genuine identity – for such, ultimately, is common lot – but the experience of a radical change of condition, the ordeal of the transition from one world to another that few human beings undergo, on account of the immobility of societies.

Complexion as *Passing*

Analysis of Pascal's deconstruction of the personal and social self helps us bring out one of the basic characteristics of transclasses – namely, passing. The whole of fragment 688 of the *Pensées* revolves around what passes – the passerby and the passing – while the *First Discourse on the Condition of the Grandees* is based on 'passing for' or 'passing oneself off'. That is why, keeping things in proportion, the dynamic of transclasses may be equated with a form of passing. The practice of passing originally spread in the United States among mixed-race blacks with a pale complexion, the 'half-bloods' who passed themselves off as white in the hope of escaping slavery and enjoying a better life. They fled segregation by exploiting their physical appearance, which enabled them to identify with the white community and mix with the right company.

In her novel *Passing*, published in 1929 and translated into French under the title *Clair-obscur*, Nella Larsen, born to a white mother and a black father who divorced before her birth, analyses the crossed destiny of two black women – Clare and Irene. Both of them can pass for white because of their skin complexion. One chooses to pass, but the other does not. Clare, an orphan whose first name is no accident, conceals her origins and gets herself married to a rich, racist white who does not know her secret – or not consciously at least, for, in one of those witticisms to which the unconscious holds the secret, he sometimes nicknames her 'Nig' in jest, observing that her skin gets browner with age. Irene, her childhood friend, marries a dark-skinned man of her race and opts to remain in Harlem, where she leads a comfortable life among the black intelligentsia. At once fascinated and disapproving, Irene, who comes across Clare by chance, asks about the practice of passing, which arouses her curiosity. Putting to one side the highly risky character of the enterprise, her questions might also apply to the transclass:

> She wished to find out about this hazardous business of 'passing,' this breaking away from all that was familiar and friendly to take one's chance in another environment, not entirely strange, perhaps, but certainly not entirely friendly. What, for example, one did about background, how one accounted for oneself. And how one felt when one came into contact with other Negroes.[20]

A hazardous business – such is passing to the highest degree, as attested by the tragic conclusion of the novel and the vigorous repression of passing in real life. At the mercy of denunciation, transgressors risked not only losing everything, swinging from freedom to slavery prior to its abolition, but met with severe penalties, especially after the Jim Crow one-drop rule in the late nineteenth century, establishing that a single drop of black blood was sufficient to legally declare someone black and require them to respect the laws under segregation, prohibiting mixed marriages and separating blacks and whites in transport and public spaces. Passing, which highlights the fallacious character of the notion of race, based entirely on a physical appearance that is, at the very least, misleading, involves a transgression of boundaries, a passing that is a 'passing oneself off'. It makes it

---

20   Nella Larsen, *Passing* (London: Penguin, 2020), p. 20.

possible to subvert the social determinism of race by crossing the colour-line, and is like a conjuring trick, denounced as a fake when it is exposed.[21]

The word *passing*, rendered as *white-passing* in Louisiana, is difficult to translate into French. The term *white-passing* does not capture the essence of passing and the multiplicity of its forms. For it is not always effected in the same direction and is not limited to blacks and whites, even though it principally concerns them. Laure Murat thus notes the case of Archibald Belaney, a white Englishman born in 1888, who emigrated to Canada and all his life passed himself off as an Apache under the Indian chief name Grey Owl. She remarks that the term *passing* was subsequently extended 'to any practice of identitarian transgression, particularly sexual, with man "passing" for woman or vice versa, gay "passing" for heterosexual, etc.'[22] It could be translated by *la passe* [passing], even though the semantic diversity of the word in French can be confusing. It involves taking the plunge, being smuggler of oneself, scaling the barriers between two worlds.

---

21 In the United States, the practice gave rise not only to significant trials but also to a whole literature revolving around the issue of passing and its tragic effects when the origins of the mixed-race persons passing themselves off as white are discovered, and their position in polite society collapses. The second half of the nineteenth century thus saw the birth of a literary genre, that of the 'tragic mulatto'. On this, see Laure Murat, 'Preface', in Nella Larsen, *Clair-obscur* (Paris: Flammarion, 2010), pp. 14ff. More recently, the theme of passing has been the subject of such accounts as *Black Like Me* (1961), by the journalist John Howard Griffin, a white man from the US South who passed himself off as black; or novels like *The Human Stain* (2000) by Philip Roth, in which the protagonist conceals his black origins to pass himself off as an American Jewish intellectual. It has also been explored in cinema in films like *Imitation of Life* (1934) and *Watermelon Man* (1970), as well as in music – particularly in the song 'Passing Complexion' from the album *Atomizer* by the group Big Black, recorded in 1986.

22 Murat, 'Preface', p. 14, n. 1.

In any event, it is clear that the neologism 'transclass' captures this dynamic of passing, of transit between two classes. In the English language, the expression 'class passing' was coined to express the phenomenon. The word *passing* is used in sociology in the English-speaking world to refer to an individual's capacity to pass herself off as a member of a social group other than her own, whether a racial or ethnic group, a social class, a community of sex, gender, or age. It can refer to a simple change of clothing by a person who wants to pass for belonging to a higher social stratum. The term is constructed out of the verbal phrases 'pass for' or 'pass as', as a forgery that passes for the genuine article or an imposter who passes himself off as someone else. It is interesting to note that the term *passing* encompasses all forms of passage, both those promoted as legitimate postures by the American dream, such as changing social class, and those rejected as shams (if only in the past), such as changes of gender or race.

However, it must be observed that in the course of history, and depending on the country, change of social class is not always regarded favourably, and is not free of all risk. Transclasses sometimes lay themselves open to vindictiveness and reprisal from those who have always regarded them as impudent intruders, and who set upon them when they make a false move. In front of his jurors, Julien Sorel recognizes the wickedness of his crime, while being perfectly aware that he is being judged not by his peers, but by 'outraged members of the bourgeoisie', and that the verdict will be biased:

> But if I were less guilty, I see around me men who have no time for any pity that my youth might deserve, and who will wish to punish in me and for ever discourage this generation of young men who, being born into an inferior class and in some sense ground down by poverty, have the good fortune to get

themselves a decent education, and the audacity to mingle in what the rich in their arrogance call society.[23]

But even when class passing is less stigmatized by public opinion and does not have the secret, risky character of racial or gender passing, it still retains a hidden aspect. For the original social origin, with its train of behaviour and habits, is covered up by subsequent developments, and is not immediately apparent. If these can show up on the surface, or be flushed out, they remain partially concealed, whether deliberately or otherwise. Class passing involves a labour of metamorphosis and social adaptation to the new milieu. And the whole question is how far integration can go.

Class-Passing between Adaptation and Non-adaptation

More than anyone else, the transclass has the feeling of having no fixed, frozen identity, but being of a floating, flexible complexion. In this regard, the absence of rigorous terms for referring to those who change class must not systematically be construed as a form of concealment or critique. It may also be interpreted as an index of the difficulty of thinking about this phenomenon, imparting a stable reality to it, and assigning it a status other than transient. The transclass is mobile in texture, characterized in the first instance by deliverance from forms of class determination. Her complexion is marked by great plasticity and a capacity to make the big move between opposed milieus. She demonstrates a remarkable form of physical and mental flexibility and an uncommon capacity to adapt.

---

23 Stendhal, *The Red and the Black*, transl. Catherine Slater (Oxford: Oxford University Press, 1991), p. 502.

To adapt is, in the first instance, to learn to discard old habits and take leave of the prevailing customs to enter an alien universe. It is a question of ridding oneself of the past, closing down assets – in short, liquidating an inheritance. This is concisely summarized by Annie Ernaux in *A Man's Place*: 'Now I have finished taking possession of the legacy with which I had to part [*déposer*] when I entered the educated, *bourgeois* world.'[24] Adaptation involves a form of deposit, even deposition, in order to get into position. It takes the form of dismissal of old values and manners and involves a self-stripping and moulting difficult to carry out all at once. That is why the transclass is necessarily going to float along in her new clothes, for she cannot adjust straight away. She is at once an adapted and non-adapted being. It is impossible for her to wipe the slate clean in one go and suspend all her behaviour by practising who knows what kind of radical doubt à la Descartes. On the one hand, she is not necessarily conscious of the displaced character of her conduct and habits – to her they seem obviously natural. On the other, however informed, she does not know the finer points of the bourgeois world's laws of propriety and etiquette. Ernaux thus registers her difficulty in understanding forms of politeness and interpreting codes:

> For a long time courtesy between parents and children remained a mystery to me. Also, it took me years to 'understand' the kindliness with which well-mannered people greet one. At first, I was ashamed. After all, I didn't deserve such consideration. Sometimes I thought they had conceived a particular liking for me. Later I realized that their smiling faces and kind, earnest questions meant nothing more to them than eating with their mouth shut or blowing their noses discreetly.[25]

---

24 Annie Ernaux, *A Man's Place* (New York: Ballantine Books, 1992), p. 100.

25 Ibid., pp. 63–4.

Deciphering signs is all the more tricky in that they are clouded by the codes of the native milieu, which interpose themselves and create a screen. Direct style, brutal frankness, restrained greetings are more conventional in popular milieus, where people speak without affectation, so that extreme affability cannot be spontaneously construed as a general norm of good manners. Instead, it seems an exceptional manifestation of attention and recognition of a particular person who genuinely merits consideration. Accordingly, what is mere courtesy or amiability can be interpreted as an expression of friendship, and this misinterpretation is a source of misunderstandings and disappointments. For polite indifference is fancifully transformed into a sign of differentiation and election. The transclass therefore has to learn to familiarize herself with an indifferent deference, to conceal her boredom under the guise of a close interest, to project the illusion of sympathy or benevolence, when she is thinking about something else entirely. She must lose her brusqueness, polish herself, and create a mask.

This is not easy, because it comes up against the persistence of earlier ways of being, like the rejection of hypocrisy, plain speaking, or direct attitudes, which derive from the habitus of the native milieu where people are less inclined to handle others with kid gloves because they believe that no one is made of sugar and spice or is superior. Not infrequently, brutal frankness, rude remarks, invective, gruffness, being loud-mouthed – these form part of the sociability of popular milieus, without anyone taking undue offence and attaching real importance to them.[26] The sons and daughters

---

26 Thus, in *A Man's Place*, Ernaux notes that her parents continually addressed each other reproachfully, even in their concern for one another: ' "Don't forget to take your muffler!" and "Why don't you sit down for a while?" sounded like insults.' She adds that they were constantly finding fault, shouting and insulting each other: ' "A nobody, that's what you are!" "And you're raving mad!" "You're pathetic!" "You stupid old bitch!" And so on. It didn't mean anything' (p. 62).

of good families, full of their own importance since birth, are so used to placing a value on their person and dignity that they find these harmless manners scandalous and outrageous when they are imported into the world of the big bourgeoisie. Transclasses must therefore come to appreciate that frankness is regarded as aggressiveness, even nastiness. They must draw a veil over their thoughts and, if they wish to avoid mortally wounding him, resist the temptation to speak home truths to a minor marquis. They enter a world where *amour propre* is king and the least pinprick to it amounts to a crime of *lèse-majesté*. In accordance with their new social environment, they must learn to appreciate what kind of bourgeoisie they are dealing with – petty, middle or big, new or old – and know how to differentiate the ethos of the world of finance or enterprise from that of intellectual and artistic milieus.

Bourdieu distinguishes the relationship to culture of the petty-bourgeois and the high bourgeoisie thus:

> The petit bourgeois do not know how to play the game of culture as a game. They take culture too seriously to go in for bluff or imposture or even for the distance and casualness which show true familiarity; too seriously to escape permanent fear of ignorance or blunders, or to side-step tests by responding with the indifference of those who are not competing or the serene detachment of those who feel authorized to confess or even flaunt their lacunae.[27]

Acquisitive man, inspired by a fear of being caught out, the petty-bourgeois conceives the relationship to culture as one of accumulation and hoarding, whereas the big bourgeois lives it in the mode of profligacy, as 'what remains when all else is

---

27 Pierre Bourdieu, *Distinction: A Social Critique of the Judgement of Taste*, transl. Richard Nice (Abingdon: Routledge, 2010), p. 331.

forgotten', and has a more casual, playful relationship with it. Out of coquetry he can confess his shortcomings, his little lies, his intellectual dishonesty, for he is well born. He is above this culture and his being is not defined by having it.[28] Similarly, the relationship of the petty and big bourgeoisie to finance is based on a very different ethos. The petty-bourgeois obeys a logic of acquisition and exhibition of his fortune. He accumulates assets, capital, ostentatiously: purchase of real estate, display of wealth and assets. By contrast, the big bourgeoisie of finance cultivates more of an ethic of discretion and is loath to publicize its wealth. It prefers income from securities to real estate that is visible, and never discloses the exact amount of its fortune.

Whatever the differences in lifestyle and variations in etiquette, it is clear that bourgeois culture inclines more to a form of inhibition of affects and, in particular, encourages curbing those that obstruct a pleasant exchange between human beings. Expressing anger or intense disagreement is contrary to the norms of decorum. In all circumstances, it is appropriate to have good manners – in other words, to behave and restrain oneself, displaying a smooth, impenetrable, polished expression. As Lampedusa remarks ironically, 'he realised how agreeable can be a well-bred man, for at heart he is only someone who eliminates the unpleasant aspects of so much of the human condition and exercises a kind of profitable altruism (a formula in which the usefulness of the adjective made him tolerate the uselessness of the noun).'[29] The violation of these norms, which are beneficial economically as well as socially, is unspeakable behaviour, revealing bad manners and a lack of education.

If she wishes to integrate into polite society, the transclass

---

28 See ibid., especially Part Three, 'Class Tastes and Life-Styles'.

29 Giuseppe Tomasi di Lampedusa, *The Leopard*, transl. Archibald Colquhoun (London: Everyman's Library, 1998), p. 100.

must therefore get rid of the sharp edges of her earlier way of being, which will gain her a reputation for being violent or awkward when she had no intention of so being and would be the first to be surprised if told she was being wounding or provocative. Such a metamorphosis requires time and a long period of maturation, for it cannot occur until she has discovered what is wounding about her own manners. In his *Sketch for a Self-Analysis*, Bourdieu emphasizes the protracted process of this dawning awareness, confessing that it took him time to understand that some of his most anodyne reactions were open to misinterpretation because of the way he expressed himself, notably by a tone, gestures, and pulling faces, with 'a mixture of aggressive shyness and a grumbling, even furious, bluntness' that contrasted with the poise of Parisian inheritors. They were taken at face value and perceived as violent, when they involved reflex, even ritual violations of the conventions of the intellectual and academic world.[30] Bourdieu also recognizes that, despite all his efforts to appropriate the codes and conform to them, his conduct betrayed the traces of a previous ethos, like the abrasiveness that authorized him to tell someone that he was talking rubbish.

Everything is indeed a question of manners, as is attested by the meeting between the rich peasant Don Calogero Sedàra and Prince Tancredi in *The Leopard*. Don Calogero, who is used to performing his actions with effective, 'Sedàra-ish' cruelty, and has hitherto regarded nobles as sheep to be fleeced, gradually grasps that the young aristocrat is as hard as he is and is achieving the same ends not by snatching but through the charm of his good manners. Unwittingly, he succumbs to this charm and registers its efficacy:

Gradually Don Calogero came to understand that a meal in

---

30   Pierre Bourdieu, *Sketch for a Self-Analysis*, transl. Richard Nice (Cambridge: Polity, 2007), p. 89.

common need not necessarily be all munching and grease stains; that a conversation may well bear no resemblance to a dog fight; that to give precedence to a woman is a sign of strength and not, as he had believed, of weakness; that sometimes more can be obtained by saying 'I haven't explained myself well' than 'I can't understand a word'; and that the adoption of such tactics can result in a greatly increased yield from meals, arguments, women and questioners.[31]

However, this learning process is not immediately profitable, for he has to assimilate the new manners. This involves a patient labour of moulding and refinement over time. The narrator observes:

> It would be rash to affirm that Don Calogero drew an immediate profit from what he had learnt; he did manage from then on to shave a little better and feel a little less aghast at the amount of soap used for laundering, no more; but from that moment there began, for him and his family, that process of continual refining which in the course of three generations transforms innocent boors into defenceless gentry.[32]

The transition from one class to another thus does not boil down to a simple theoretical assimilation of habits and habitus. It requires their incorporation into practice – what Bourdieu calls learning through the body.

To change class is to enter an alien world whose language has to be learned, signs deciphered, and forms of behaviour embraced. To adapt is to adopt a language, assimilate values, appropriate representations, which can be bewildering in their foreignness. It is to submit one's body and mind to constraints that clash with rooted habits, meeting with their resistance, to

31 Lampedusa, *Leopard*, pp. 100–1.
32 Ibid., p. 101.

the extent that acquiring a posture can be a form of torture. Change of class is the discovery of a *terra incognita* not only to be deciphered but to be cleared, for one must plough one's own furrow and undertake cultivation in accordance with the requisite norms of sowing. It resembles an ethnological experiment, but of a particular kind, for the transclass is intent on joining the tribe and exposes herself to rejection. She is therefore both observer and observed, operating under evaluative scrutiny. In this respect, if she can play at being Lévi-Strauss on a small scale, she also knows that she is a Nambikwara or a Persian in Paris, and is going to be subjected to various rites of passage and integration. The ceremonial of the first meals in the bourgeois world therefore has more of the initiation rite about it than the ethnological delight. The proliferation of glasses and cutlery appears not so much a sign of magnificence and refinement as an occasion to multiply errors of taste. The transclass therefore has as much to fear from the objects around her as the subjects. She is subject to the court of words she must know how to use and of things she must know how to handle.

To penetrate the bourgeois world is not simply to be confronted with beings who are polite in a different way from you. It is to make an incursion into a universe of objects that are the natural appendices of wealth, culture, and distinction, and which plunge the transclass into an abyss of perplexity, sometimes putting her in a spin. The greater the deprivation of the native milieu, the more considerable the effort required to adapt and the more numerous the grounds for humiliation. How to confess that one does not know how to telephone, flush a toilet, use a shower, switch on a TV – to say nothing of the more sophisticated apparatuses and countless technological inventions that adorn wealthy dwellings? Such inability is literally inconceivable, and there is a strong risk of its passing for idiocy or backwardness.

The transclass therefore sets about concealing her

incompetence, struggling against objects, and foiling their traps. She is thus condemned to a sort of experience of premature ageing – that lived by elderly people completely overwhelmed by the modern world and severed from others, because they do not know how to use the cohort of recently invented objects defining the new forms of conviviality, to demonstrate the technological mastery that is the precondition for integration. Ultimately, it is also the world of class objects that resists her effort to adapt. Rejected by people, rejected by things, the transclass is often vulnerable to the transplant's failure to take.

She is therefore always on alert, for she risks being caught out and put in a position of failure and inferiority. The upshot is a form of secret anxiety or self-doubt that can find expression even in a tendency to boast of successes and result in inhibited or self-censoring behaviour. The latter can show up in an inability to put oneself forward or to allow oneself to cross certain thresholds of social promotion.

Events are therefore an occasion not so much for demonstrating that one is at ease as for overcoming unease, so that a happy outcome gives birth to contentment (*gaudium*) rather than self-satisfaction (*acquiescentia in se ipso*), to speak in Spinozist terms. Whereas self-satisfaction is a joy born from human beings contemplating themselves and their power of acting, contentment is a joy accompanied by the idea of a past thing that has happened contrary to every expectation.[33] *Gaudium* is therefore the form of joy implying that a form of sadness has been dispelled.

Consequently, the complexion of transclasses is a blend of audacity and timidity, combativeness and inhibition, which are the product of a torn history and attest to the constant fluctuation between adaptation and non-adaptation. This

---

33 Benedict de Spinoza, *Ethics*, ed. and transl. Edwin Curley (London: Penguin, 1996), Book III ('Of the Affects'), p. 108.

affective complex does not pertain to character traits, but is the fruit of class transition and is commensurate with the gap between conditions.

The complexion of transclasses is thus like a 'complexation' or the formation of a chemical complex. It resembles a combination in which a molecule, a counter-ion of opposite sign, is added to a central ion or molecules, uniting with it to form an entity where the properties of these molecules or ions are concealed. Far from a simple identity, we are dealing with a combination of opposites, a mixed contexture, but which does not necessarily appear such under the impact of integration.

In reality, transclasses are two-faced, like Janus Bifrons, the god of doors, one of whose faces is turned towards the past, the other towards the future. But, depending on whether the doorway is more or less open or closed, the old face remains in the shade or materializes again – sometimes mobile, when the past shows on the surface, and sometimes fixed, when it is repressed. Characterized by mobility and successive moultings, the transclass is defined by a *transidentity*, and subject to a logic of the in-between.

2 The In-Between

Whatever her desire to sever her ties, the transclass is always attached to an origin, whether she acknowledges it or not. The ties may be tenuous or loose, but the native bond cannot be completely broken; despite denegation and dissimulation, a transclass cannot negate the fact that she was born where she was born. Integration into a different world is not a point of no return. For one is always referred back to one's origins, if only when the death of parents reminds everyone that they are someone's child; that they issued from those parents, despite everything; and that they are part of a lineage and a history which have fashioned their initial complexion and continue to act on them against their will. There is no age for being an orphan. The death of parents reawakens the traces of the child slumbering in the adult, handing down an inheritance in relation to which she must situate herself, if only to refuse it. It is probably no accident that Annie Ernaux wrote *A Man's Place* after her father's death, or that Didier Eribon wrote *Returning to Reims* after the loss of his.

That is why, even if the transclass takes on the colour of the place where she sets herself down, to speak like Montaigne, her contexture is always a tincture. She cannot deny her mutation and claim to retain her native colour in full, for any return home carries the patina of the distant stay or the invisible varnish of the detour. The transclass is thus characterized by a twofold affiliation: she is in the middle of milieus, at the intersection, in the in-between.

This dual affiliation is strikingly brought out by the ritual of alternating suits established by the Marquis de la Mole in *The Red and the Black* to regulate his delicate relations with Julien Sorel, who is at once his inferior, as a private tutor, and his equal, since he has raised himself to his table through ambition and love. The Marquis de la Mole supplies a blue noble's suit to Julien Sorel, which is a counterpart to his black commoner's suit. According to whether Julien opts to wear one or the other, the marquis treats him differently. In his blue suit, in the colours of the aristocracy, he is a blue blood and treated by the marquis as an equal, with exquisite politeness. In his black suit, in the colours of the lowborn priest, he is the employee, the secretary addressed as an inferior:

> One day the marquis said in the tones of excessive politeness that often irked Julien:
>
> 'Allow me, my dear Sorel, to make you a gift of a blue suit: when you see fit to don it and to call upon me, I shall regard you as the younger brother of the Comte de Chaulnes, that is to say the son of my friend the old duke.'

Julien did not really understand what was going on; that same evening he tried out a visit wearing a blue suit. The marquis treated him as an equal. Julien had a heart worthy to appreciate true politeness, but he had no idea of nuances. He would have sworn, before the marquis had this whim, that it was impossible to be received by him with greater courtesy ...

... The following morning Julien presented himself to the marquis in a black suit, with his briefcase and his letter to be signed. He was received in the old manner. In the evening, with a blue suit, the tone was quite different, and every bit as polite as the day before.[34]

Yet complexion does not come down to the alternation of nuances, for Julien is also black under the blue suit and blue under the black suit. Cleavage is not the only form of division. Variegation can display itself as posture, blurring as image, or diversity as quality. Whatever its figures – graft or tincture – complexion resembles hybridization. Weaving is an interbreeding. But, instead of by birth, it is formed by cutting and stitching and, if well done, nothing but blue is to be seen in it. The complexion of the transclass is formed in the course of a history and of changes that amount to neither a superimposition of strata nor the substitution of one for another. Its constitution does not obey any laws of successive temporality conducive to estrangement from the native milieu for the purposes of gradual rapprochement with the novel milieu.

Naturally, it is possible to distinguish stages such as distancing from native milieu, adapting to a new way of life, and assimilation to the novel milieu. But the transition from one condition to another is no linear progression. It is accompanied by ebbs and flows where the past returns in the present

---

34 Stendhal, *The Red and the Black*, pp. 285–6.

and transforms it in turn. It would be a mistake to think that the native milieu corresponds to the world of childhood; that the years of transition and learning occur in adolescence; and that perfect integration into the new world happens in adulthood, possibly giving way to reversion when retirement beckons. These distinct phases do not follow one another systematically, but overlap, develop correlatively, and are mutually supportive.

Thus, the discovery of new ways of life can as easily be the cause as the consequence of distance from the native milieu, and vice versa. Integration does not occur without a crisis, when the boomerang of origins brings back a past that does not pass – and it is perhaps never fully effected. As to returning, it does not necessarily have the form of the odyssey of reappropriation referred to by Bourdieu in *The Bachelors' Ball*.[35] When relations with the family have not been broken off, it can involve a constant toing-and-froing; or it might never occur, in favour of voluntary or forced forgetting.

The *Ethos* of Distance

Whatever their subjectively lived modalities, transclasses are objectively characterized by what might be called an *ethos* of distance, a way of being forged through the practice of passing and the experience of the in-between. At the crossroads between two worlds, they experience a double distance, from the native milieu and from the novel milieu. This distance does not necessarily come down to an equidistance or the search for an ideal point of equilibrium. It can manifest itself in varying degrees of proximity and distance, depending on the differences between individuals and the gap between their

---

35 Pierre Bourdieu, *The Bachelors' Ball*, transl. Richard Nice (Cambridge: Polity, 2007).

respective milieus of origin and arrival. The scale of the journey and the nature of the distance are not obviously the same, whether the transclass is leaving a deprived rural milieu for a remote big city or a nearby suburb where she has already been able to rub shoulders with difference and incorporate certain cultural codes, whether she escapes a black ghetto to live in a world of comfortably-off whites. Representations of this difference also vary for the same individual in the course of her history, her trajectory most often resembling a chaotic hybridization and not a form of continuous progress, involving completely stripping oneself of earlier conventions and conduct to adopt the postures of the milieu like a second nature.

The *ethos* in question is born in the first instance from a distance that can be characterized as *private* and *internal*. This distance presents itself as the introduction of an I and an interplay that convey or betray a sort of detachment – a decentring from the original condition – and resemble a displacement on the spot, for it is mental in kind, not physical. Nizan describes its premises in *Antoine Bloyé*:

> And that very evening, as he sits on his doorstep, Antoine awkwardly begins to feel that the world to which his studies are impelling him, and toward which he is driven by childish ambition, is considerably removed from the world where his parents have lived since their youth. He feels the beginnings of estrangement. He is no longer quite of their kith and station. He is already unhappy as though after a farewell, an irrevocable breach of faith . . .[36]

This distance takes the form of an affective separation, before taking effect and being marked by a real change of class. This

---

36 Paul Nizan, *Antoine Bloyé*, transl. Edmund Stevens (New York: Monthly Review, 1973), p. 53.

is what also emerges from an arresting passage in *A Man's Place*, where the train journey acts as a metaphor or symbol for social trajectory. The author becomes aware of her new class affiliation while thinking about the fact that she is travelling first class and that the change is irreversible:

> I suddenly realized with astonishment: 'Now I really am *bourgeois*,' and 'It's too late now.'
>
> Later that summer, while I was waiting for news of my first job, I thought to myself: 'One day I shall have to explain all this.' What I meant was to write about my father, his life and the distance which had come between us during my adolescence. Although it had something to do with class, it was different, indefinable. Like fractured love.[37]

What is objectively called 'class distance' cannot render the singular emotional charge of subjectively lived distance, of fractured love that constricts the heart, the irremediable loss of affection and symbiotic complicity, but also of rejection and the refusal to resemble one's family, bound up with a sense of being other or radically different.

For subjectively lived class distance does not systematically assume the shape of an endured, painful estrangement. It can be a willed, assertive estrangement expressing a contemptuous desire not to be like one's siblings, pride at being different, assurance of success and confirmation of superiority. This emerges, for example, from John Edgar Wideman's confession to his brother in *Brothers and Keepers*: 'One measure of my success was the distance I'd put between us.'[38] Didier Eribon also adopts this in his case, when he assigns one of his brothers the implicit role of reference-point for what he does not

---

37 Ernaux, *A Man's Place*, pp. 14–15.
38 John Edgar Wideman, *Brothers and Keepers* (Edinburgh: Canongate, 2018), p. 38.

want to be and is distancing himself from, fleeing through him the working-class world to which he already no longer belongs.[39] Ultimately, however, it is perhaps always a question of fractured love, since it often seems that detachment and the refusal of any family resemblance refer to a part of oneself that one does not love and that one has erased.

This internal distance is rapidly compounded by an external distance. Initially mental, it becomes spatial when internal malaise translates into remote migration. *Déclassement* invariably occurs through displacement, so true is it that two worlds cannot coexist in the same space and occupy the same camp. Consequently, historical change of class presents itself as a geographical remoteness, crossing a frontier, separating town from countryside, capital from province, the centre from suburbs, upmarket suburbia from dormitory towns, developed countries from developing ones, and so on. Julien Sorel leaves his native Verrière for Besançon, and then goes up to the capital. While Annie Ernaux moves from Yvetot to Rouen, going up to Paris becomes the sign of social ascent for many. Rastignac's cry could rally many transclasses. But the phenomenon is not peculiar to France. The distance John Edgar Wideman puts between himself and his brother is one that separates the black ghetto in Pittsburgh from Pennsylvania University in Philadelphia. Changing classes, changing places.

The transclass is allocated a new residence after her transfer. She experiences a class transportation, and her journey resembles a form of transhumance or immigration. That is why she appears as a transfuge or, more precisely, an internal immigrant, to adopt Ernaux's terminology.[40] This formula,

---

39 Didier Eribon, *Returning to Reims*, transl. Michael Lucey (London: Penguin, 2019), p. 105.

40 Annie Ernaux, *L'Écriture comme un couteau* (Paris: Stock, 2003), p. 35.

which the writer uses by analogy with external immigration to think about her trajectory within French society, renders the dual dimension of the distance – geographical remoteness and mental disorientation – and the internal exile experienced by the transclass, because she is separated from those who were once her people while sometimes being a thousand miles away from her new milieu.

The *ethos* of distance concerns not only class of origin but also class of destination. Martin Eden attests to it straight away, because at every turn he is confronted with the otherness of the bourgeois world, so that everything becomes a sign of the gulf separating him from Ruth. Thus, for example, seeing his mother leave a bank becomes 'another proof of the enormous distance that separated Ruth from him'.[41] She belongs to the class that has dealings with bankers. This distance is represented on several occasions as a gulf – the one separating the crude, gross universe of the sailor from that of legitimate, refined culture, which the transclass wants to bridge without knowing what walkways to take. It is the clash of worlds that opens up a breach in the limited imaginary of the transclass and causes him to measure the distance to be travelled to abolish the difference and appropriate what he naively covets, idealizing it.

Very often, the experience of being allowed to enter a wealthy dwelling for the first time is the occasion for this realization of an unimaginable gap between ways of life. It assumes the aspect of a violent revelation, for the transclass sees difference, puts his finger on it, and cannot believe his eyes. In this respect, Martin Eden's narrative is exemplary, for many transclasses have a similar experience, sometimes fooling themselves (as they later discover) about the degree of wealth, culture, and refinement for want of any comparative scale and discrimination:

---

41 London, *Martin Eden*, p. 47.

> I was never inside a house like this ... I'd heard about such
> things an' read about such things in some of the books, an'
> when I looked around at your house, why, the books come
> true. But the thing I'm after is, I liked it. I wanted it. I want it
> now. I want to breathe air like you get in this house – air that
> is filled with books, an' pictures, an' beautiful things, where
> people talk in low voices an' are clean, an' their thoughts are
> clean. The air I always breathed was mixed up with grub an'
> house-rent an' scrappin' an' booze ...[42]

The years of learning and the work of metamorphosis might
be defined as an enterprise of spatio-temporal absorption of
difference, because the endeavour consists not simply in filling
a gap, but in catching up. The transclass sets about devouring
books in sometimes bulimic fashion, and to frequent sites of
culture assiduously. Abolition of the distance is thus lived on a
model at once topological and chronological, so that the
career of the transclass involves overcoming obstacles and a
race against time, plugging gaps, and acquiring knowledge in
a rush.

But once the gap has been reduced and the biggest lacunae
filled, the *ethos* of distance is going to continue to govern her
conduct in the world of arrival, for her new habits have been
acquired and do not possess the natural obviousness they
have for those in the groove, who have no memory of having
learned them. Although this might be imperceptible to an
external gaze, the transclass is not part of things from the
outset, but often slightly withdrawn and, as it were, on the
fringes. For she is scarred by a need always to maintain her
distance and give herself time to observe the codes, so as to
adjust and avoid faux pas. She can thus seem to be forever on
her guard, for she cannot identify spontaneously with things
and coincide with them, unlike those used to believing they

---

42 Ibid., pp. 60–1.

were made for them. The distance of the observer sometimes renders her more her own spectator than an actor. She watches what others are doing, and what she is doing, with the lag peculiar to conduct that pertains less to reflex than reflection. What will be identified as gaucheness or awkwardness is an expression of this hesitation and self-dissociation, which paradoxically leads to joining the circle while remaining on the fringes.

The transclass is like the ideal duke educated by Pascal. He cannot confuse his being with his condition; he always has a backward glance and a forced lucidity. Even when he is blind about himself, he vaguely knows that he is not of this world and must suppress doubts about his legitimacy. When he occupies a position of power or is appointed to a position for which he was not destined by birth, he cannot completely stick to his role and perform it comfortably, as if it were his due or a natural extension of himself, like an inheritor who is at one with it and does not distinguish between being and having. Thus, he can act contrarily to what is expected of him, for he cannot conform to the prevailing model because of his ambivalent relationship with it. He hails from the world of the dominated, and cannot identify with a dominant position unreservedly or uncritically.[43]

Thus Bourdieu, who occupied an eminent position in the intellectual world, did so while often taking an opposing view to the dominant models in the field. He states that his ambivalence towards the intellectual world

is the generative principle of a *double distance* ... a distance from the great game of French-style intellectual life, with its

---

43 This is also observed by Didier Eribon, who highlights that distance from a role is probably a less easy position to adopt than perfect coincidence with one's professional or social status. See his *La Société comme verdict* (Paris: Fayard, 2013), p. 43.

fashionable petitions, its demonstrations *du jour* or its prefaces for artists' catalogues, but also from the great role of professor, engaged in the circular circulation of thesis juries and examination boards, the games and stakes of power over reproduction; a distance, in politics and culture, from both elitism and populism.[44]

This awkward posture of non-coincidence with one's social role holds out the precious possibility of withdrawal and critical distance. A position of strength, which can help take the wind out of the sails of power and alter the lines of domination, but also a position of weakness, which can lead to self-scuppering when the transclass who is a victim of impostor syndrome is resistant to herself and prohibits herself from adhering to what she does. She must, so to speak, struggle to be what she is. This is doubtless also one of the reasons why some transclasses, in a kind of legitimist reflex, are *plus royalistes que le roi*, over-acting roles and functions to prove that they are up to them. The desire to show that they rightly belong to the new social class translates into a kind of pious reverence for its rules and values, which leads to their being applied literally, without any sense of perspective.

Transclasses then become pillars of institutions, models of conformism, or caricatures of the world they wish to join, after the fashion of the *bourgeois gentilhomme* who exposes himself to ridicule, or the Verdurin whose salon exudes vulgarity to the aristocratic nose of the Guermantes. Whereas the person familiar with the codes for ages knows how to operate them flexibly and can allow herself minor violations that will earn admiration, the transclass, who does not possess this facility, is inclined to follow them strictly and to exhibit rigidity. She is then transfixed in a role and reveals that it is not

---

44   Bourdieu, *Sketch for a Self-Analysis*, p. 107.

really made for her, to such an extent does she overdo things, transforming a posture into a parody. Class arrogance can be more pronounced in commoners who have risen socially than in native-born bourgeois. For it involves keeping anything that recalls origins at a distance and offering guarantees of belonging to the new milieu by developing a strategy of borders and radical demarcation. Far from being confined to a form of haughty indifference, it can take a hateful, explicitly contemptuous turn. The transclass then overdoes it and struggles to find the right distance. But, whether too far removed or too close, the issue is always distance. The transclass is never in the right place; she is always out of place, displaced, in search of her rightful place.

Besides, distance is not only experienced in the inner self, but is marked from the outside and signified by the attitude of those who are bourgeois by origin. It is not only felt; it is made to be felt. Thus, Martin Eden is kept at a distance by Ruth, even though she is attracted by him, as indicated by the ambivalent scene where, 'at the piano, she played for him, and at him, aggressively, with the vague intent of emphasizing the impassableness of the gulf that separated them'.[45] The transclass strives to break down distance, the legitimate inheritor to preserve it, by crushing with her scorn the bastard who is a pretender to the throne or mocking the ridiculous quirks of the parvenu. Class arrogance leads to the interpretation of difference as inferiority, and equation of the desire to ascend socially with a form of grotesque arrogance. The will to distinction refers to what Nietzsche calls the 'pathos of distance', which aims to establish a hierarchy and differentiate according to ranks.[46] 'The higher *should* not reduce itself to an instrument of the lower, the pathos of

---

45   London, *Martin Eden*, p. 21.
46   Friedrich Nietzsche, *On the Genealogy of Morals*, transl. Douglas Smith (Oxford: Oxford University Press, 1998), p. 12.

distance *should* keep even their missions separate to all eternity!'[47] The will to distinction is therefore nothing other than the attempt to maintain an imaginary separation by introducing a symbolic distance, which acts like a cordon sanitaire intended to preserve the dignity of a social status and prevent the devaluation bound up with the extension of privileges to commoners.

Even when the transclass is readily received into polite society, admiring astonishment at her exceptional career, and praise for her merits and pugnacity, make her feel the full extent of the distance between those who 'only have to take the trouble to be born' and those who must win places in a hard-fought battle. She is admitted to the catch-up like an outsider who goes to the front, and she owes her integration to the largesse of a benevolent circle, which is afforded an opportunity to salve its bad class conscience and exhibit a spirit of tolerance and openness to social diversity. The transclass remains a survivor, even a prodigy or exotic curiosity sometimes smugly exhibited in salons so that she can recount her incredible story before people tire of it and move on to the next thing. So unstable is her foundation that she is not really of this world; she belongs to it not by birth but by chance. No permanent seat, in short, only a place on credit.

But nor does she belong to the world of her origins, even should she seek to rediscover her roots. The transclass is no longer the same; her complexion has altered. The counterpart of the distance of departure bound up with remoteness is a distance of return bound up with rapprochement. Far from savouring of reunions, encounters with the world of old are often like missed rendezvous, and are the occasion for measuring the increase in the divide. In transit between two worlds, Martin Eden registers it bitterly when he comes across comrades

---

47   Ibid., p. 103. Emphasis in original.

from the world down below – the gardener, the gardener's assistant and stable hands, with whom he eats in haste without their having much to say to each other: 'he realized how far he had travelled from their status. Their small mental caliber was depressing to him, and he was anxious to get away from them.'[48] Martin Eden recognizes that he can bridge the gulf created by books without difficulty, because having lived in the working-class world, 'the *camaraderie* of labor was second nature with him'.[49] Nevertheless, when he joins back up with his old gang, and has the impression of living again and becoming human again in toasting with them, he is aware that he has irrevocably changed and reached a point of no return: 'the beer seemed not so good as of yore. It didn't taste as it used to taste. Brissenden had spoiled him for steam beer, he concluded, and wondered if, after all, the books had spoiled him for companionship with these friends of his youth.'[50]

Paradoxically, to get closer is to take the measure of the estrangement. If geographical distance can be bridged, historical distance cannot be completely abolished. One is reversible; the other is not. The transclass is no longer on an equal footing in this once familiar world. Here too she is displaced. Between her and the others there will always remain the difference between those who left and those who stayed. Thus, she experiences the fate of immigrants returning to their native land: she is a stranger in her own country. She can perfectly adapt to it and cultivate the *ethos* of distance, to the point of transforming it into a pathos of difference. Triumphant return to the native milieu then amounts to a simple detour the better to reach the destined milieu and confirm an acquired position, by calling as witnesses those who have remained to make them guarantors of one's own

48   London, *Martin Eden*, p. 143.
49   Ibid., p. 142.
50   Ibid., pp. 356–7.

118

superiority. The parvenu who struts around exhibiting conspicuous signs of economic or cultural success in her native milieu is the inverted variant of the *bourgeois gentil-homme*. One says, 'I'm one of you', proclaiming it to the face of the nobles; the other says, 'I'm not one of you', throwing it in the face of the ignoble.

Should the transclass end up forgetting it by chance, the natives make a point of reminding her. She was from here but lives elsewhere and, to have a residence permit, must prove that she has remained a local child – that she is not a traitor. The transclass must therefore offer guarantees of belonging, mould herself into the old suit, forget the young brother of the Comte de Retz, and become Julien Sorel, erasing all traces of the blue suit. The task is not an easy one, for the transclass is put under question and commanded to answer if she is still part of the family and the milieu, and her words and deeds are scanned for signs of adherence or renunciation.

From this point of view, the case of the Antillean who left for the metropolis and then returned home analysed by Frantz Fanon in *Black Skin, White Masks* can serve as a paradigm for understanding the ordeal of the transclass:

> The Antillean returning from the *metropole* speaks in Creole if he wants to signify that nothing has changed. It can be sensed on the docks where friends and relatives are waiting for him – waiting for him not only in the literal sense, but in the sense of waiting to catch him out. They need only one minute to make their diagnosis. If he says: 'I am so happy to be back among you. Good Lord, it's so hot in this place; I'm not sure I can put up with it for long,' they have been forewarned – it's a European who's come back.[51]

---

51   Frantz Fanon, *Black Skin, White Masks*, transl. Richard Philcox (New York: Grove, 2008), p. 20.

News of the return fuels the expectation of those who stayed – expectation of the one who was missed, for he left; expectation of the one who is distrusted. The issue is whether the person who arrives is an arriviste; whether he thinks he is or has remained one of us. He is therefore awaited with bated breath, all the more so because his departure has sometimes been experienced as a renunciation, rejection, or abandonment; and there are often things to make those who left you pay. When he approaches, he is criticized for having moved away. He is in a state of conditional reintegration and must guard his tongue and his conduct so as not to be accused of having gone over to the enemy. He must therefore be at a remove from himself, partially concealing what he has become in order to be recognized.

This distance fosters a profound malaise because the transclass is no longer adjusted to the world he used to live in, and must engage in contortions such as playing his own role, reincarnating the child or adolescent he once was, passing over his mutation in silence. This constitutes a big gap wherein the person dresses up as a character to deliver an expurgated version of herself acceptable to the audience. If she is a good actor, the transclass can fool herself and rediscover the pleasure of slipping into old clothes. She can also suffocate under the mask and feel dispossessed in making herself the actor of her past life, rather than being the agent of her present existence.

In numerous accounts by transclasses, reintegration occurs at the cost of self-censorship or denial of the change by the native milieu. In particular, this denial manifests itself in profound ignorance of the novel milieu of the transclass – ignorance in the dual sense of both not knowing and scorning it, which is reflected in the form of absence of genuine curiosity and inquiry about that milieu, beyond a few pieces of information confirming one's image; or in the form of enjoyment mixed with resentment to hear it denigrated in celebration of the superior world of those who stayed put.

The world of origins is evasive in its turn, for the nostalgic desire to re-join one's class is as mythical as the dream of returning home dear to immigrants. In truth, one does not return to Reims, one goes back to it like a ghost. The transclass is, in the strict sense, a revenant. She no longer exists for those who stayed, unless it be in the spectral form of the one who left, or the revenant who sometimes wanders over old ground before vanishing again. A ghost from the past, she haunts the places of yesteryear in search of a lost self, and struggles to find embodiment in the new world, for she comes from afar. She is in transit and lives in inter-worlds, like Epicurus's gods, but often does not possess their glorious indifference, for her complexion is a complexion under stress.

Fluctuatio animi: A Complexion under Stress

Sometimes on the other side of the big gap is a tear, a separation. Caught in a vice between two divergent social worlds, the transclass is frequently buffeted, finding herself prey to what Spinoza calls *fluctuatio animi*, or 'vacillation of mind'.[52] *Fluctuatio animi* refers to the state of mind engendered by two opposite affects. It is an expression of ambivalence and, as long as the conflict is not absorbed, it induces hesitation and swings from one condition to another. The transclass is the bearer of two worlds, and is haunted by a dialectic of opposites without any guarantee that they might be harmonized and that the oscillations might resolve into some kind of equilibrium. The coincidence of opposites underlies what Bourdieu calls the 'cleft habitus'.[53] If this habitus, which is

---

52   Spinoza, *Ethics*, Book III, proposition 17, scholium, p. 80.
53   Bourdieu, *Sketch for a Self-Analysis*, pp. 100ff. See also Pierre Bourdieu, *Science de la science et réflexivité, Cours du Collège de France*

constructed out of a dual experience, such as election to the educational aristocracy and popular origins, inclines to the reconciliation of opposites, tensions persist bound up with the discrepancy between lofty consecration and humble social extraction. Condemned to the big gap between often incompatible worlds, a transclass is necessarily worked on by open or subterranean contradictions. Having lived and shared the history of the dominated, she has passed to the other side of the barrier and now belongs to the world of the dominant. She experiences the class struggle in herself and is, so to speak, her own enemy. Desire is now a cleavage faced with the surrounding milieu: to be part of it or not to be – such is the question.

However, the transclass must not get the problem wrong by believing she has to make a decision to place herself in one of the camps. For she is not trapped in the alternative of the 'either/or', but rather in the logic of 'neither/nor' or 'both at once'. She is neither wholly proletarian nor wholly bourgeois, since she is no longer exactly what she was and is not exactly what she has become. Even if she is intent on expressing class solidarity and identifying unreservedly with either her old condition or her new one, she must adopt a hybrid position and be aware of her situation.

If, for example, she claims that she has remained close to the people, she risks passing them by while thinking she is fighting at their side. This is the mistake made by certain intellectuals hailing from the popular classes, who began to speak in the name of the people and reduced them to silence by sometimes giving them lectures without attending to their

---

2000–2001 (Paris: Raisons d'agir, 2001): 'To avoid indefinitely overloading the analysis, I would like to come back to what seems to me the main point: the fact that the contradictory coincidence of election to the educational aristocracy and popular, provincial origin (I would like to say: especially provincial) underlay the constitution of a *cleft habitus*, generator of all sorts of contradictions and tensions . . .' (p. 214).

demands. It is always risky to speak in place of others, especially when one no longer occupies their place. The risk is in
confusing the aspirations of an enlightened fringe, however
legitimate, with those of the people as a whole – failing to take
account of the difference of positions, and confining oneself to
postures of incantation and admonishment that are the opposite of genuine solidarity.[54]

But if registering a position can dispel misunderstandings, it does not thereby abolish tensions. A complexion
that unites opposites is vulnerable to conflicts that are
expressed, in particular, by ambiguous attitudes to the
native and new milieus alike. As regards the milieu of
extraction, the transclass is pulled between contradictory
affects, which by turns prompt her to reject or rehabilitate
it. She thus oscillates between forms of shame and scorn for
the native milieu and a certain pride and loyalty, swinging
from hatred to love and love to hate in abrupt reversals
between for and against.

If she is intent on breaking completely with her milieu and
maintaining a watertight separation, she will be induced to
return to it, if only in the fleeting form of a sense of guilt; and
she exposes herself to the forceful return of the repressed.
Accounts are never definitively settled, for her debts just about
catch up with her and she cannot draw a line under them.
Setting aside cases of extreme maltreatment or total abandonment, transclasses owe their careers partly to the sacrifices

---

54 Ignorance of difference of position thus leads to the denunciation of workers who sell themselves to the bosses for a meagre wage
increase, as opposed to striking and making the revolution, or castigat-
ing their simple-minded racism and political errors, rather than understanding their causes and finding effective means to remedy them.
Transclasses are generally no longer in a situation where the same family,
economic, and social burdens weigh on them, such as the procession of
mouths to feed, the indebtedness that strangles, or the painful constraints
of neighbourhood. Thus they may well play the beautiful soul and dream
of an ideal people that is always combative and generous.

made by their family, which has sometimes worked hard to pay for their education, as attested by Michel Étiévent:

> I always saw my mother every day creating her children's future, writes Duras. I never saw mine sit down for a single moment. Peasant, housewife, she put everything into our lives to try to make us love the future. I remember her washing for hours on end in the icy water of the ponds. Day after day, laundry after laundry, at the tip of hands distorted by chilblains, she was paying for the words I bought at the bookshop. Today still, when I choose a work, I think of her. Her hands come back to me, hands that never had the time or the strength to hold a book. The words I write today belong to her. I write in order to repay.[55]

The awareness of such sacrifices is acute and unforgettable. The debt is inscribed on the body of the other, in the worn-out hands of workers, in the tired bodies of peasants, in all those folds and creases of the face wherein the history of rough work and poverty can be read. Unless of utterly bad faith, the transclass cannot ignore the price of things and the effort they cost. Michel Étiévent thus evokes a pregnant memory: 'One day I stole five francs from my mother. She didn't say anything to me. She simply showed me her hands. At the time five francs amounted to six hours of hands soaked in freezing water.'[56]

His case is far from isolated. Most transclasses experience this sense of being bound by an enormous, crushing debt. Didier Eribon likewise feels himself in debt, despite rejecting the milieu on which it is based. In particular, he stresses the sacrifices of his mother who had to flog herself to death for

---

55 Michel Étiévent, *Aux silences de l'aube* (Paris: Éditions Gap, 2006), p. 86.
56 Ibid.

eight hours a day in a factory so that he could follow courses on Montaigne and Balzac at the lycée, or remain shut up in his room deciphering Aristotle and Kant at university.[57] He also recalls Annie Ernaux's terse formula in connection with her mother in *A Woman's Story*: 'I was both certain of her love for me and aware of one blatant injustice: she spent all day selling milk and potatoes so that I could sit in a lecture hall and learn about Plato.'[58]

Whether or not she is certain of her family's love, the burden of the debt and the unjust fate of those who have sacrificed themselves necessarily weighs on the conscience of the transclass. In the ingratitude of forgetting or the gratitude of remembering, she is caught in the grip of guilt and has difficulty escaping it. She often lives like a miracle survivor and, when she looks back on her past, can have a sense of having unjustly benefited from a privilege and be tormented by the bad conscience of being a survivor, when so many of her co-pupils, who were just as worthy, have been eliminated, victims of social selection. She is thus plunged into a to-and-fro motion between leaving and returning, remembering and forgetting.

Her feelings about her new milieu can be just as antithetical and mixed. Divided between fascination with the refinement and repulsion at the frivolity, envy at the comfort and contempt for the casualness, admiration in the face of distinction and anger over arrogance, the transclass is agitated by opposing movements of attraction and hostility. Paradoxically, she can evince the utmost humility and utterly inordinate pride because she is simultaneously subject to a sense of illegitimacy and the assurance of possessing genuine legitimacy, since she owes her place exclusively to merit, not to some birth right. At once below and above inheritors, she is in an

---

57   Eribon, *Returning to Reims*, p. 80.
58   Annie Ernaux, *A Woman's Story*, transl. Tanya Leslie (New York: Quartet Books, 1990), p. 54.

untenable posture that prompts her to place herself on the fringes.

But in playing with boundaries, she does not escape the torment of the dialectic of the inside and the outside, which derives from the contradictory desire both to conform to the rules and to violate them. The transclass embodies the impossible figure of the rebel conformist. She wants to be accepted and recognized by polite society but cannot tolerate being integrated. Having long complied with the requirements of bourgeois culture and the norms of literary language, Martin Eden discards his success and, addressing Ruth, vehemently denounces the world he has idealized:

> 'The bourgeoisie is cowardly. It is afraid of life. And all your effort was to make me afraid of life. You would have formalized me. You would have compressed me into a two-by-four pigeonhole of life, where all life's values are unreal, and false, and vulgar.' He felt her stir protestingly. 'Vulgarity – a hearty vulgarity, I'll admit – is the basis of bourgeois refinement and culture. As I say, you wanted to formalize me, to make me over into one of your own class, with your class-ideals, class-values, and class-prejudices.'[59]

Fruit of the *fluctuatio animi*, the contradictory posture of the rebel conformist is not a mere novelistic figure. In his *Sketch for a Self-Analysis*, Bourdieu shows how the cleft habitus is the source in him of ambiguous, contradictory behaviour: docility and indocility. On one side, the application and submission of the good pupil lead him to comply with the rules of the academic game. On the other, a restive disposition, particularly towards the education system perceived as an ambiguous *alma mater* – object of probably excessive love and revolt based on indebtedness and disappointment – impel

---

59   London, *Martin Eden*, p. 394.

him into dissidence and incite 'the temptation to spoil the game', to disrupt the institutional ritual, during exams or solemn occasions such as prize-giving, inaugural lectures, or thesis juries.[60] The same phenomenon is reproduced at the level of affective dispositions. On the one hand, a form of modesty, bound up in particular with the 'insecurity of the self-made parvenu', which leads him not to disdain humdrum tasks, and to invest as much care and interest in directing an interview as in developing a theoretical model. On the other, 'the lofty self-assurance of the *miraculé*, who comes to see himself as "miraculous" and is inclined to challenge the dominant on their own ground'.[61] Bourdieu thus confesses that, as early as École normale, many of his options were determined by 'a form of aristocratism, not so much arrogant as desperate'. It was the result of retrospective shame at having sacrificed to the game of the competitive exam, a reaction against 'the "good students"', and a species of self-hatred bound up with rejection of the petty-bourgeois social climbing embodied by some of his fellow pupils, parvenus at the summit of the university hierarchy, who had become perfect models of the *homo academicus*.[62]

These contrary affects, deriving from the situation of the in-between, are not necessarily experienced by all transclasses in mechanical fashion. They are generated in response to circumstances when the conditions of their realization are given, and are not lived with the same intensity if combined with affects that temper and counteract them. Given a complexion particularly marked by *fluctuatio animi*, the transclass will soon be inclined to be wounded or wounding, and risks being perceived as touchy or aggressive if she is not careful. She can find herself labelled as a bad-tempered or

---

60 Bourdieu, *Sketch for a Self-Analysis*, p. 101.
61 Ibid., pp. 101–2.
62 Ibid., p. 102.

tempestuous character, as if it was a question of a personality trait when what is involved is a disposition bound up with a situation. Without mentioning misunderstandings, tension reaches a peak when the transclass passing from confusion to contempt cultivates provocation and plays the prole in the bourgeois world or the bourgeois in the company of proletarians. She thereby carves her black sheep statue by exaggerating opposites, but this display figure does not inhibit tensions. Instead of veiling them, it unveils and confirms them.

Given the uniqueness of histories and the unprecedented character of situations, an a priori inventory of the forms of contrariness inherent in the complexion of transclasses is probably futile, doomed to failure. It is, however, possible to focus attention on certain common features of tension born of the in-between, which play a key role in the dynamic of self-constitution, whatever their various lived modalities.

First and foremost comes social shame, which (as we have seen) can play either a motivating or an inhibiting role in the dynamic of non-reproduction, by inciting either rebellion or submission. Shame is one of the most constant affective markers in the career of transclasses. It persists even when the transclass has extricated herself from her native milieu, like some indelible trace of infamy that no success can completely erase.[63] It is the prototype of the tenacious affect that indefinitely feeds off itself and cannot stop. It has the potential to produce its opposite, so that tension reaches a climax and the subject is torn apart – not only is she ashamed; she is ashamed to be ashamed.

This is the experience described by Camus in his largely autobiographical book *The First Man*, when he recounts little Jacques's discovery of class differences and his mother's

---

63 This also applies to other forms of shame, such as that linked to homosexuality, as Didier Eribon recalls in *Returning to Reims*, pp. 216–17.

reification under the ignominious category of 'domestic'. Jacques, whose father (like Camus's) is dead, has to fill in forms about his parents' occupation, and does not know what to put down for his mother:

> At first he put 'home-maker' while Pierre put 'post office employee'. Pierre explained to him that home-maker was not an occupation but was said of a woman who kept her own home and did her own housework.
>
> 'No,' said Jacques, 'she takes care of other people's houses, especially the shopkeeper across the street.'
>
> 'Well,' Pierre said hesitantly, I think you have to put down "domestic".'
>
> That idea had never occurred to Jacques, for the simple reason that this all-too-rare word was never spoken in his home – and this for the reason that no one there had the feeling that she was working for others; she was working first of all for her children. Jacques started to write the word, stopped, and all at once he knew shame and all at once the shame of having been ashamed.[64]

The sudden realization that, in the eyes of the world, his mother is a 'domestic', and occupies a subaltern rank, devalues her, and makes him feel ashamed. But this bad feeling rebounds against him, for he scorns himself for ratifying, if only on paper, that social judgement of the person he loves and who sacrifices herself for him.

Consequently he is ashamed of being ashamed, and his suffering is intensified by a rage at himself. If shame indicates estrangement, the shame of shame reveals proximity, and that is, no doubt, why Camus specifies that 'his mother as she was remained what he loved most in the world, *even*

---

64 Albert Camus, *The First Man*, transl. David Hapgood (London: Penguin, 2001), p. 159.

if that love was hopeless'; as if he could no longer reach her and had lost her after this twofold fault: her failure and his own failure.[65] The shame of shame intensifies the original shame like a power to the second degree, without suppressing it by a reflexive balancing movement, which displaces it from the other onto oneself and from oneself onto the other. Jacques *simultaneously* experiences shame and shame at having been ashamed, for (Camus tells us) he is discovering the judgement of the world 'and, with it, his own judgement on the hard heart that was his'.[66] Thus, his shame is reproduced in a closed circuit and multiplied, for everything becomes a reason for recalling it, including the guilt of experiencing it. It triggers a motion of *fluctuatio animi* that seems interminable: Jacques does not escape shame, but brings it into himself.

To understand why the complexion of a transclass is built up, and comes undone, around social shame, we must analyse the mode of production of this stubborn affect, its peculiar dynamic, and the configurations that derive from it. In general, shame is a feeling of disgrace generated by condemnation of a thought, an act, or a way of being which, rightly or wrongly, is considered bad. Although it can have multiple sources, it always involves the representation of a gaze that gauges and judges, regardless of whether that gaze is external or internalized.[67]

Indeed, shame is not necessarily the internal impact of a moral condemnation formulated by others. Most often, it is based on imagining a disapproving external gaze, such that the subject sees herself with the eyes she attributes to others, and would like to hide or disappear underground. But she

---

65 Ibid., p. 160. My emphasis.
66 Ibid., p. 159.
67 On this point, see Vincent de Gaulejac, *Les Sources de la honte* (Paris: Desclée de Brouwer, 1996).

cannot, because she is split in two: at once judge and judged, she cannot extricate herself. That is why Spinoza defines shame as 'a sadness, accompanied by the idea of some action which we imagine that others blame', and does not reduce it to the effect on us of external censure.[68] This does not mean that shame is purely imaginary and baseless. It is based on the presence of incorporated images and traces, bound up with moral judgements inculcated by family and society, which go on confusedly producing effects in us and are incessantly reactivated, even in the absence of external censure.

Consequently, it is not enough for others to declare that there is nothing to be ashamed about, or to evince signs of esteem, to dispel shame. For the person who feels shame remains marked by a degraded image of herself, which persists as long as another image does not succeed in supplanting it. No reason on its own suffices to destroy an affect, because it is rooted in a physical and mental alteration whose traces are borne by the body and mind. That is why Spinoza stresses the fact that true knowledge of what is really good or bad cannot, just by virtue of being true, suppress an affect.[69] It is efficacious only if it is itself an affect. It is therefore futile to seek to demonstrate to someone else that she is not shameful by means of well-turned arguments, for she will not be touched by them. Like any affect, shame can only be counteracted or destroyed by a more powerful contrary affect.[70]

The same schema obtains in the case of social shame. The transclass is embarrassed by her origins, for she imagines, rightly or wrongly, that others deem them inferior; and she has internalized this judgement. Thus, when confronted with her native milieu in the presence of an alien third party, she

---

68 Spinoza, *Ethics*, p. 109.
69 Ibid., p. 123.
70 Ibid., p. 120.

can experience a profound unease, for she perceives things with the condemnatory gaze she attributes to others. Whereas the experience might leave the bourgeois indifferent, since he is foreign to this universe and not directly implicated, the transclass is on tenterhooks and feels threatened: she identifies, and fears being identified despite herself, with her former milieu. She looks at herself in the way she imagines the bourgeois looks at her, and feels shame at the idea not only that her native milieu is deemed inferior, but that she is judged by way of a milieu to which she no longer belongs, but with which she is nevertheless identified. Shame feeds off fear of the amalgam, and betrays an impossible desire to distance oneself.

Social shame is a paradoxical affect, involving both detachment from and attachment to the native milieu. Detachment, because the subject sees things with a certain sense of perspective, adopting the assumed standpoint of the superior milieu and applying its codes. Attachment, because she feels responsible for her parents and their environment, and assumes their putative faults or defects as if they were her own, or as if she had been irremediably contaminated by contact with social pariahs. Shame evinces attachment in the form of a stain or blemish. It relies on a degraded image of the self and those close to her, a confused representation that transforms a fact into a fault, denying its necessity and acting as if it resulted from a perfectly free choice attributable to an agent responsible for her errant ways. Shame is a confession of guilt, and is sustained by the belief in free will with its train of mortification and self-flagellation.

Transclasses can thus blacken their milieu from time to time without necessarily being conscious of it, so that their autobiographies are sometimes subject to sharp criticism and furious protests from family and friends, who do not recognize themselves in the unflattering portraits of them in the bleak painting describing their living conditions. However, the distorted perception the transclass might have of her own history expresses the truth of the affect – that of shame and indelible humiliation.

In reality, no one should feel social shame, because no one is responsible for their origins. And it is just as absurd to criticize someone for being born into a 'bourgeois' or 'prole' family as to stigmatize them for their large or small size. But this common-sense argument carries no weight in the face of the suffering created by the conviction of one's own indignity, for social shame is not a mere reflection of an objective situation of degradation, but is also fed by fictive representations that go on generating real effects even when the reasons for opprobrium have been removed. In this it obeys the same rules as other forms of shame. To fight it, we need to understand how this imaginary has been able to take shape, and dismantle the mechanisms of its formation by investigating the social genesis of shame.

The imaginary of social shame is based chiefly on an interpretation of class difference and of the subordination of the dominated in terms of the inferiority and baseness imputed to them. In the first instance, it is rooted in registration of the gap between ways of life and social practices, and is constituted on the basis of the transition from being to value. In other words, the conversion of an ontological judgement into a value judgement presides over the birth of shame. In short, social pride or shame are born once different milieus stop being described and instead are proscribed, or prescribed, as base or elevated living conditions. What is becomes subject to what should (or should not) be, divided into what possesses value and what does not. Instead of being irrelevant or amounting to a disparity that could be corrected by justice, difference becomes inequality, and is expressed in terms of superiority and inferiority. Under the impact of a comparison, it is converted into a sign of distinction and hierarchy. In the absence of any comparison, there is no social shame, only misery or want.

The question is where this surreptitious slide from being to value, which makes all the difference in the world, comes from. In reality, it is imposed. It is the ideological expression of power relations, and results from the domination of one class over another, from the desire to perpetuate it combined with a bad conscience, which leads all faults to be imputed to the dominated, securing their consent through subterfuge or persuasion. The imaginary of social shame is the historical product of the division of society into classes and, by this token, goes beyond the private framework of a given consciousness, be it that of a transclass or some other individual. It is an avatar of the class struggle in the theoretical field and, more precisely, the result of ideological formations that express, underpin, and perpetuate social hierarchy on the terrain of ideas. Political hierarchy is transformed into natural order by means of education, culture, the press, and all the means of communication capable of manufacturing opinion, so that the dominated internalize the idea that they are inferior beings, lazy or untalented, who belong to the 'world down below', born to obey and be led. Less wealth, less culture, less power, less than nothing!

This is the bedrock in which class prejudices are rooted and the stigmatization of popular strata develops. So-called lower classes are labelled with derogatory labels: 'hicks', 'hayseeds', 'slobs' for peasants; 'proles', 'rednecks', 'chavs' for workers. The former opposition between the noble and ignoble, manservants and villeins, is succeeded by that between VIPs, the great of this world, and the 'little people', the ordinary folk who are not persons, look like a mob, and lack class. The *populo cracra* replaces the swinish multitude; the words change, but the humiliation remains. The current tendency to euphemization, or the proclamation of the disappearance of the working classes in favour of middle classes, conceals this opposition, but does not abolish it. In this respect, the negation of the existence of classes with different interests emerges as the ultimate ruse of the dominant to maintain undivided power, and as the most insidious form of violence against the dominated.[71]

The imaginary of shame thus pertains to what might be called a metaphysical conjuring trick that consists in transforming an accident of history – the fact of domination – into an essence preceding existence and imbuing it in advance with its share of baseness. The dominated internalize domination to the point where it seems natural to them and their inferiority is like a birth mark, a stamp of infamy impressed for eternity. Shame is based on incorporating abjection that has become an immutable essence.

This phenomenon of essentialization prior to existence is not peculiar to social shame. It occurs in exacerbated fashion in the case of racial or sexual shame. Frantz Fanon shows that the lived experience of the black is always framed by a racial epidermal schema – a figure of the Negro – which precedes all being in the world. Whether he discovers existence under the seal of 'dirty negro!', or difference under 'Look! there's a negro', he is imprisoned in a crushing objectivity, a being for the white. He describes this experience ironically in *Black Skin, White Masks*: 'I was responsible not only for my body but for my race and my ancestors. I cast an objective gaze over myself, discovered my blackness, my ethnic features; deafened by cannibalism, backwardness, fetishism, racial stigmas, slave

---

71 It is clear that denial of the existence of social classes in the name of an alleged universality of the human condition is a position that often reveals affiliation to a privileged world ignorant of differences and conflicts. Criticizing Raymond Aron, who claimed that the reality of class consciousness had not been proved, Didier Eribon observes that 'as the child of a worker you experience in your very flesh the sense of belonging to the working class', and that 'the absence of the feeling of belonging to a class is characteristic of children of the bourgeoisie. People in a dominant class position do not notice that they are positioned, situated, within a specific world (just as someone who is white isn't necessarily aware of being so, or someone heterosexual)'. Eribon, *Returning to Reims*, pp. 93–4.

trades, and above all, yes, above all, the grinning *Y a bon Banania*.'[72]

Eribon likewise states that to discover his homosexuality, to become gay, was to join a category previously defined by insults: 'The stigmatized identity precedes you, and you step into it, you embody it, you have to deal with it in one way or another.'[73]

Shame carries an imaginary of the 'maculate conception', and ultimately pertains to a theological view of the world marked by original sin. Social shame is the sin of origin transmitted by parents, like an indelible stigmata – the always visible stain, even when no one sees it. It marks all actions, including those intended to erase it, and feeds off itself in amplifying itself to infinity, as indicated by the episode in *A Man's Place* where Annie Ernaux recounts the visit to her family by two of her university friends, well-mannered young women, whom her father has set his mind on warmly welcoming, bending over backwards: 'My father treated these visits as a special occasion because he wanted to honor my friends and show them that he had manners. Instead he only managed to show he was inferior, a fact which they instinctively acknowledged by saying, for instance, "*How's it going*, sir?" '[74]

The father's effort to live up to the occasion, far from erasing the shame felt by his daughter, intensifies it despite herself. Initial discomfort at her friends' potentially condescending attitude, which Ernaux averts by warning them that in her house 'it's very *basic*', is compounded by her father's behaviour, which makes her ashamed. For instead of being himself and avowing his modesty by behaving normally, he wants to

72   Fanon, *Black Skin, White Masks*, pp. 93–4.
73   Eribon, *Returning to Reims*, p. 192. See also Didier Eribon, *Réflexions sur la question gay* (Paris: Flammarion, 2012).
74   Ernaux, *A Man's Place*, p. 83.

be different and starts to ape the bourgeois, covering himself in ridicule without realizing it. A maladroit attempt to better himself irremediably replicates baseness, as an awareness of inferiority cannot surface. Indeed, it assumes comparison with a different milieu and an in-depth knowledge of its codes in order to appropriate them.

This is indicated immediately after this passage when a remark is made by the father, who one day says to his daughter with a proud look: 'I have never given you cause for shame.'[75] This self-proclamation, which might seem like a denegation and betray a form of self-doubt, invites the daughter to acquiesce and to repress the shame she has experienced. There is nothing like it to make her ashamed of having been ashamed, and to turn the affect back against herself in an endless cycle. For shame summons shame, giving the impression that it will never stop, as Ernaux senses.[76]

It is endlessly fuelled by new reasons, and contaminates every act, past and future alike, for it is felt retrospectively or in advance. It is not confined to the gaze focused on the native milieu, but also attains the new milieu by ricochet. On the one hand, transclasses feel ashamed to confirm the 'between ourselves' of the bourgeois world; to maintain a complicit silence, rather than taking up the defence of the popular classes; to form part of a smug, blind caste all of whose lived experience and openness to the world boil down to sometime crossing the rue d'Ulm to get to the rue de la Sorbonne – in a word, to betray. On the other hand, she is ill at ease and embarrassed if by chance she introduces lovers and friends from elevated spheres into her native milieu, for she is afraid that her own embourgeoisement – in a word, her betrayal – will be condemned through them.

---

75 Ibid.
76 Ibid., p. 102.

She is therefore subject to the crossfire of social judgement, and is sometimes doubly ashamed – of her family, which is commonplace, and of her new friends, which is less so. Shame at posh friends is, so to speak, inverted shame – a mirror-image shame rooted in their ignorance of the social codes that obtain in popular milieus and their inappropriate behaviour. They use overly refined language and cannot hit upon the right words; they waste food, leaving, for example, what is fat; they are reluctant to finish dishes; they are incapable of getting their hands dirty, and so on – so many faults of taste and lack of manners, which will lead to their being taxed with being wealthy, spoilt children and parasites. Shame is never-ending and must be drunk to the lees!

Experienced more or less intensely, depending on people's particular histories, and the various narcissistic wounds that can reinforce it, this affect produces remarkable effects such as censure, avoidance, denial, or disavowal, especially of the native milieu. Frequently, transclasses remain silent or highly elliptical about their past, are embarrassed saying what their parents do, or are evasive in discussions of their family and siblings. They sometimes pretend not to know former acquaintances when they encounter them by chance, or are very ill at ease and keep unavoidable meetings short, particularly when accompanied by their new acquaintances. Didier Eribon confesses that he was terribly embarrassed when asked what his brother did, and that he always managed not to tell the truth.[77] He also mentions his chance meeting in the centre of Paris with his grandfather, a window cleaner, when he was 'acutely embarrassed, terrified that someone I knew might see me with him, perched on top of his strange contraption'.[78]

Keeping things in proportion, this fear of being seen in bad company, of having one's origins unmasked, which leads to

---

77 Eribon, *Returning to Reims*, p. 103.
78 Ibid., p. 68.

being constantly on the look-out and engaging in conceal-ment, is one of the characteristics peculiar to 'passing'. In Nella Larsen's novel of that name, Clare, who has disavowed her race to pass herself off as white, lives in a state of constant dishonesty and terror of being found out and denounced. Although she likes to play with fire, the visits she cannot prevent herself making to her old black friends in fear and trembling are clandestine. In a way, the transclass is also a clandestine figure: she hides herself to see, or not to see, her family, in order to preserve a fragile, threatened identity. The shame of origins and the fear of being found out can lead to major adjustments to the truth, to making up stories, to improbable detours.

Without going into a detailed analysis of the innumerable figures of shame, it is interesting to note the frequent appear-ance of one of its remarkable avatars – namely, the legend of the new birth, which represents the paroxysmal form of disa-vowal of origins. If transclasses for the most part set about hiding their social origins, limiting themselves to untruths by omission, they sometimes end up falsifying them by creating a family romance that surrounds their birth with a halo of mystery and wonder. Not only is the change of milieu lived as a second life, or a veritable birth, but from time to time it is accompanied by the myth of the foundling, the orphan, the natural son of illustrious people, or the fantasy of being born without a father or mother, even of being self-made. Mythomania then becomes mythology.

The many facets of this imaginary of origins, worked on and fashioned to the point of becoming reality, are explored magisterially by Stendhal in *The Red and the Black*. Julien Sorel first imagines that he is 'a sort of foundling, hated by my father, my brothers and my whole family'.[79] But this fanciful idea does not only germinate in his head. It is adopted by Abbé

---

79   Stendhal, *The Red and the Black*, p. 37.

Pirard, who doubts the origins of his protégé: 'He is said to be the son of a carpenter from the mountains round our way, but I'm more inclined to believe that he's the illegitimate son of some wealthy man.'[80] Doubts about filiation are converted into a strategy of disavowal that culminates in the acknowledgement of Julien's high birth by an adoptive father, the governor of Besançon. At the conclusion of an arrangement with the Marquis de la Mole, who cannot consent to his daughter marrying a commoner, Julien changes his name; he stops calling himself Sorel and becomes the chevalier de la Vernaye. The choice of an adoptive family and a new patronym thus enrol Julien in a different lineage. This recognition is a rebirth and a retroactive rewriting of history that completely strikes out his father, to the point of transforming him into a simple foster parent who must be recompensed for his care. The Marquis de la Mole, having made a present of 20,000 francs to Julien, fixes the terms of the agreement thus: 'M. Julien de La Vernaye will be assumed to have received this money from his father, to whom there is no need to refer otherwise. M. de La Vernaye will perhaps see fit to give a present to M. Sorel, a carpenter in Verrières, who cared for him as a child.'[81] Julien ends up convincing himself that this ennoblement is not a borrowed identity, but a form of reparation that restores his true origin, or at least confirms him in his sense of deriving from a high lineage and not being the son of his father: 'Could it really be possible, he wondered, that I might be the natural son of some great lord driven into exile in our mountains by the terrible Napoleon? This idea seemed less improbable to him with every passing moment ... My hatred for my father would be proof of it ... I shouldn't be a monster any more!'[82]

---

80 Ibid., pp. 222–3.
81 Ibid., p. 464.
82 Ibid., p. 465.

The invention of a different origin or a new birth is not confined to the novel. Over and above daydreaming or story-telling to mislead the company, it sometimes transpires in reality via judicial procedures of adoption and change of name. Some transclasses have themselves been adopted by their parents of choice even though their biological parents are still alive. This kind of adoption can be inscribed in a movement of an existentialist kind, intent on asserting a radical freedom to choose, including parents. If man is what he makes himself, he is not determined by his past; he chooses himself and invents his family. The true family is not the one imposed by nature, but the one chosen knowingly. In this conception, there is no biological family, but only philosophical families. This idea did not remain purely theoretical, but was given juridical expression in practices of legal adoption. For example, Jean-Paul Sartre and Simone de Beauvoir resorted to adoption – the first of Arlette Elkaïm, the second of Sylvie Le Bon, both of whom took their respective names, even though their parents were alive.

Yet, however legitimate, we may ask at what point this voluntaristic practice of adoption by transclasses is not a ruse of shame and a subtle form of disavowal of origins. Why should it be necessary to choose a new family, from the moment when it is possible to create a circle of relations for oneself, among whom older or younger people can figure who are capable of being role models or model friends?

Similarly, we can examine whether the ideology of the self-made man is not also tinged with a shameful desire to erase the traces of origin, even though that is not its principal motivation. For a man, however powerful, does not make himself all on his own, by himself. Although they express a positive desire to take one's own existence in hand and transform it, the idea of self-creation or the fashionable desideratum of self-fashioning might likewise be suspect in this regard, when presented as an attempt to wipe the slate clean and start all over again. For nothing is made out of nothing, but always out of a history. Thus, the concern to sculpt oneself *ex nihilo* is perhaps the ultimate form of a burning shame sublimated into a work of art. Yet no one is fooled in reality. It always involves unmaking oneself just as much as making oneself, working on a material that has been previously shaped. It is therefore important to recognize the material's texture if one wishes to be able to alter it. Even artists have debts, and the transclass always vaguely knows that she must pay hers. That is why she oscillates between shame and shame at being ashamed, which possibly represents one of the first forms of acknowledgement of debt and the beginning of pride. The issue is how to make shame go away, escaping the 'vacillations of the mind' that trigger mental turmoil.

Divided between detachment from and attachment to the old world, between allegiance and resistance towards the new, the transclass is traversed by fluctuations that derive from the in-between. Accordingly, the whole problem is to pass from a floating complexion to a fluid one, which tensions glide over.

Being Oneself through the Other

The in-between posture is scarcely comfortable. As a result, some transclasses, haunted by doubt, wonder if they would not have been happier staying at home, and end up regarding change not as self-realization but as a form of perdition. Far from being an elevation or promotion, social ascent can be lived as a protracted descent into hell. Martin Eden is an exemplary instance of this. An exile in two worlds, he does not really belong to either of them, and lives in a no-man's-land where he feels alien to himself and others to the point of dying from it:

He could find no kinship with these stolid-faced, ox-minded bestial creatures. He was in despair. Up above nobody had wanted Martin Eden for his own sake, and he could not go back to those of his own class who had wanted him in the past. He did not want them. He could not stand them any more than he could stand the stupid first-cabin passengers and the riotous young people.[83]

Martin has lost his Eden; he experiences the decline and abandonment of those who have left the mythical world of origins without any possibility of returning, and who are consumed by a vain nostalgia. He 'vainly hark[ed] back to forecastle and stoke-hole in quest of the Paradise he had lost. He had found no new one, and now he could not find the old one.'[84] His suicide simply consummates the failure of the search for a self never found or forever lost. Martin is already dead to himself, for life has long since deserted him.

This tragic end brought Jack London criticism, particularly from Mayakovsky, who was to alter it when he wrote the screenplay for the film *Creation Can't Be Bought*, based on the novel. The film does not end with the hero's suicide, but 'shows us Ivan Nov, that is, Eden, who manages not to succumb under the weight of the gold in which he is covered'.[85] Two years after Jack London's controversial suicide, Mayakovsky, who would in turn put an end to his life, could not reconcile himself to the idea that 'Martin Eden the rebel, and his double, Jack London the socialist, could have lacked revolutionary faith to the point of giving in to an act of nihilistic despair'.[86] No doubt fears of political repercussions might

---

83   London, *Martin Eden*, p. 407.
84   Ibid., p. 407.
85   Lili Brik, *Avec Maïakovski* (Sorbier, 1980), quoted in Linda Lè, 'Préface' in Jack London, *Martin Eden* (Paris: Phébus, 2001), p. 12.
86   Lè, 'Préface', p. 13.

lead to passing in silence over the profound unease of trans-classes, which is expressed not only in suicide but also in serious depression and personality disorders. It might be feared that such a tragic fate could dampen ardour and license inertia. Does not Julien Sorel end up on the scaffold? These fears, moreover, are not unique to communists or progressivists in general. They can be shared by liberals or conservatives, anxious to utilize a certain social mobility as a safety valve. What is to be done if the American dream turns into a nightmare?

At all events, it is clear that change of class cannot automatically be equated with an improvement in living conditions and construed as a positive development. It can be the source not only of great suffering, but of alienation. How not to get lost in transition and how to overcome the shattering of a fragmented complexion? The real difficulty is to become oneself like an other, and not as an alienated figure. Alterity or alienation: such is the stake of the alteration involved in transfer.

Michelet is probably one of the first to have posed the problem. He observes that 'they who rise, almost always lose by it; because they become changed, they become mongrels, bastards; they lose the originality of their own class, without gaining that of another. The difficulty is not to rise, but in rising to remain one's self.'[87] Social ascent is therefore a misnomer; far from being synonymous with elevation and systematic gain, it nearly always ends in loss. The transformation involved in changing class is presented not as progress, but as decline, a bastardization. The transclass is short-changed because he ceases to be original and metamorphoses into a copy. He is diminished, becoming a shadow of his original class and a pale reflection of his new class. This is what Michelet asserts in the

---

87 Jules Michelet, *The People*, transl. Charles Cocks (London: Longman, Brown, Green & Longmans, 1846), p. 13.

second part of his book, when he cautions against the *effets pervers* of social ambition:

> This peasant of whom we are speaking – this man, so circumspect, so wise, has, however, one fixed idea; it is, that his son must not be a peasant, but must rise and become a citizen. He realises his idea but too well. This son, who finishes his education, and becomes *Monsieur le Curé, Monsieur l'Avocat*, or *Monsieur le Fabricant*, you will easily recognise. Ruddy, and of a hardy race, he will fill everything, occupy everything, with his vulgar activity; he will be a great talker, a politician, a man of weight, of grand views, who has no longer anything in common with humble people. You will find him everywhere in the world, with a voice drowning everything, and concealing under the finest white kid glove the coarse big hands of his father.
>
> I express myself badly; the father had strong hands, the son has big ones. The father, doubtless, was more muscular and more shrewd. He was much nearer the aristocracy. He did not speak so much, but it was to the purpose.
>
> Has the son risen higher in quitting his father's condition? Has there been progress from one to the other? Yes: no doubt, in regard to cultivation and knowledge; but not so in regard to originality and real distinction.[88]

'Bastardy' is the fruit of mixing between classes, and is accompanied by a kind of degeneration. Symbolized by the transition from the strong hands of the father to the big hands of the son, for Michelet it is linked to a loss of popular vigour and vitality, which are ablated in the one who rises and deprive him of the form of aristocracy bound up with mastery of a craft. The parvenu runs a high risk of being nothing but a vulgar bourgeois, a big mouth and red in the face, with a peasant's build but without the work capacity. The loss is not made

---

88   Ibid., p. 89.

good by acquiring knowledge and culture that will make him a semi-scholar, invariably inferior to bourgeois fine minds, and will not suffice to impart originality and unparalleled distinction to him. Accordingly, he represents a sort of median figure between the classes, bordering on mediocrity. That is why the mixing and rapid, crude blending of classes can only be sterile in Michelet's view: 'will this class of all classes, this spurious mixture which has been composed so quickly, and which is already dwindling away, ever be productive? I doubt it. The mule is barren.'[89]

Let us be clear: what Michelet castigates are 'spurious mediocrities', and not remaining oneself.[90] He does not criticize the desire for social ascent and the aspiration to improve living conditions as such, but standardization in the name of equality and the disappearance of originality under cover of diversity. That is why the problem is not so much rising as not losing (oneself). Thus, according to Michelet, people can assert their strength and remain themselves, rising or not rising: 'a strong mind can rise or descend with equal ease'.[91] Michelet would willingly believe that

> in the time to come great originality of invention will belong to men who will not be lost in that spurious mediocrity in which all native character is enervated. Strong men will be found who do not want to rise; who, being born of the people, will wish to remain of the people. To rise to a comfortable position, all well and good; but to enter the [bourgeois] class, and change their condition and habits, will appear to them any thing but desirable; they will feel assured that they would gain little by it.[92]

---

89 Ibid., p. 90.
90 Ibid., p. 91.
91 Ibid.
92 Ibid.

No doubt, it might be objected to Michelet, diversity is not necessarily synonymous with bastardy, and there are fertile, original hybridizations. But this would be unfounded, for what he especially pinpoints is the mediocrity derived from median figures erasing strong characteristics and sharp edges. In this respect, it must be acknowledged that he is not wrong to condemn unthinking promotion of social ascent as a panacea, since it can engender conformism, develop a herd mentality, and be just as much a source of alienation as of liberation. Does the combative worker who defends the rights of labour really gain by becoming a foreman and the boss's guard dog? It is not so obvious that changing class is a gain, including when it involves leaving the ghetto to become an academic and writer.

Thus, in *Brothers and Keepers*, the same John who, on the strength of his success, returned to Pittsburgh to see his superiority confirmed, confesses: 'I thought I was running away, but I was fashioning a cage', and imprisoning himself in a series of roles and masquerades, losing his authenticity.[93] At times, he even feels a form of jealousy of the dignity of Robby, his brother condemned to a life behind bars, who gets an engineering diploma in prison that he will never be able to use: 'Were my visits to prison about freeing him or freeing myself from the doubt that, perhaps, after all, in spite of it all, maybe my brother has done much more with his life than I've done with mine . . . Does what he's achieved in the narrow confines of a cell mock the cage I call freedom?'[94] This is a genuine question; and it is very difficult to answer. Is the place of a writer at the height of his fame really always superior to that of an inmate from the ghetto who seeks to educate himself, and who proudly 'show[s] the world that all [he] needed was a skill', to quote

---

93 Wideman, *Brothers and Keepers*, p. 46.
94 Ibid., pp. 283–4.

Robby's words during the award of the diploma?[95] No doubt we should dispense with value judgements, comparisons, and hierarchies, to take into account each person's power of acting, and regard what each person does in the place they find themselves in as the main thing. In this perspective, beyond good and evil, what matters is the endeavour to liberate the self and others, not the fact of rising or not rising.

Indeed, the question is not so much whether the game is worth the candle, whether it is preferable to leave one's social milieu or remain in it. In any event, changing class does not present itself in the form of an alternative or a free choice of life, but is the result of a necessity. The desire to leave or remain is simply the translation of combined internal and external forms of determination, not the expression of a contingent decision between undifferentiated possibilities. It is therefore pointless to seek to prescribe norms of choice, for the transclass obeys her own necessity. Far from the school debate about preferences, the only relevant question, consequently, is how the person who has embarked on the adventure of passing can avoid foundering and go beyond mere floating.

For Michelet, the answer consists in a formula: it is necessary to 'remain oneself'. There's the rub; and it becomes difficult to follow him. One could only remain oneself by presupposing a 'self' given as a prior reality. In these circumstances, we can ask what is the nature of this mysterious 'self' that is to be preserved. For the historian, the answer is not in doubt: to remain oneself is to remain of the people. Yet the problem is not thereby resolved, but only displaced. In accepting that the people has a nature which must be preserved in social ascent, Michelet attributes to it a kind of eternal essence which, to say the least, is debateable.

---

95   Ibid., p. 339.

In fact, he attributes to the people an instinct he never precisely defines, gifts that manifest themselves in a form of vitality, warmth, simplicity, and genius, which are to be found in the child in particular.[96] Thus, he forms part of a populist current and will help fuel the whole mythology of simple people and little people, endowed with infallible instinctive faculties, with a naturalness and an innocence that are to be preserved from corruption and degeneration, or revived historically in a harmonious society. This mythology, based on belief in an authentic popular nature, is rooted in a religious imaginary: 'Who are you, poor simple ones? The younger brothers of the eldest born of God.'[97] The genius embodied by the people in its poverty and simplicity is proximate to the figure of the saint or Christ, who proclaims: 'Suffer the little children to come unto me.'

Michelet's thought is thus marked by a perfunctory essentialism. It is based on naive, moralizing fictions like class reconciliation through love and marriage between rich and poor, and on the surreptitious transformation of historical characteristics into innate physical and moral qualities. For example, the combativeness acquired by struggling to survive on a daily basis is interpreted in terms of natural vitality, as if it were in the genes. The solidarity and mutual aid that frequently exist among the popular classes are construed as natural kindness and warmth, whereas they are forms of behaviour developed in a situation of want in order to survive, in the absence of other resources. Solidarity is the poor person's money; and there is nothing surprising about its being less widespread in the affluent classes, who can do without it.

---

96 Michelet, *The People*, Part II, where Michelet studies the 'instinct of the people'; Part II, Chapter iv, 'The Simple – The Child the Interpreter of the People'.

97 Ibid., p. 116.

To remain oneself is to remain of the people? But a given popular or bourgeois substantive self no more exists than the self *tout court*. It would therefore be more accurate to say that the most difficult thing when rising is not to remain oneself, but to be oneself – or, rather, to become it. It is clear, moreover, that one is not born popular, but becomes so at a pinch through the fashioning of collective habitus. There is no one single people, but peoples that are born and transformed in the course of history. Any essentialization runs the risk of turning the singular figure of a given people into a universal expression of the people. Michelet did not avoid this mistake, for his populism was compounded by a patriotic nationalism, tinged with anti-Semitism and xenophobia, which led him to regard France as the eternal essence of the revolutionary people condemned by Europe, or as 'a living brotherhood'.[98]

Given this, why refer to Michelet? While his approach is more that of a patriotic moralist than of an historian or philosopher, it is not without interest. Despite its mistakes, it demonstrates the need to forge mythologies in order to be able to weave a new complexion. Michelet constructs a lyrical figure of the people, a genius rising and transforming society with faith and ardour, and rehabilitates the world down below, according it a grandeur and potential capable of restoring its

---

98   See the letter to Edgar Quinet of 24 January 1846, in Michelet, *The People*: 'One people! one country! one France! Let us never become two nations, I entreat you. Without unity, we perish. How is it that you do not perceive this? Frenchmen, of every condition, every class, every party, remember well one thing! – You have on earth but one sure friend, France! Before the ever-enduring condition of aristocracies, you will always be guilty of one crime, – to have wished, fifty years ago, to deliver the world. They have not forgiven it, nor will they ever forget it. You are always their dread. Among yourselves, you may be distinguished by different party names; but you are, as Frenchmen, condemned together. In the face of Europe, know that France will never have but one inexpiable name, which is her true, eternal designation, – The Revolution!' (p. 16); ibid., p. 148.

pride and reawakening the energy needed to live and fight. Changes are not fostered by mere rational political analysis. They rely on imaginary representations that fuel hope and confidence in one's own strength and value. This imaginary is a highly useful strategic weapon, initially at least. Indeed, one of the first enemies to be conquered is self-shame, which induces withdrawal and resigned depletion. Evil comes from shame and its pedlars. As a matter of priority, we must therefore strive to free ourselves from it, as Nietzsche asserts in *The Joyful Science*:

273 *Whom Do You Call Bad?* Those who always want to put others to shame.
274 *What Is Most Humane?* To spare someone shame.
275 *What Is the Seal of Liberation?* To no longer be ashamed of oneself.[99]

In this respect, the transition from deadly shame to a salutary shame at shame is a first step. But it is not enough. To dare to hold one's head high again, one must be proud of oneself. If an affect can only be vanquished by a more powerful contrary affect, great shame can only be driven out by great pride. That is why real change first of all takes the form of a change of imaginary, in order to burst the locks of inhibition that prevent people speaking up and acting. As the Stoics pointed out, in a situation of powerlessness the only thing in our power is our representations. It is therefore a question of changing one's inner drama, converting negative pictures into positive self-images and transforming weakness into strength.

This work of subversion is rooted in the first instance in a reversal of values. Nietzsche thus stresses that 'the slave revolt

---

99 Friedrich Nietzsche, *The Joyous Science*, transl. R. Kevin Hill (London: Penguin, 2018), p. 173.

in morals begins when *ressentiment* itself becomes creative and ordains values'.[100] In this instance, we are dealing with an ethics not of action, but of reaction that 'says no to an "outside", to an "other"'.[101] Even so, it produces values and inverts representations, declaring good what opponents deem bad, and sometimes ends up imposing itself.[102] But whether we are dealing with a negative *ressentiment* that begins by inventing a villain and devaluing the other in order to re-value the self, or with a pure affirmation, 'a triumphant affirmation of [one]self', it is a question of being conscious of one's own forces and forming a more glorious self-image.[103] Generally, reconciliation with oneself involves rehabilitating the shameful part, and takes the form of what Goffman calls inverting the stigma – that is, embracing signs of abasement as emblems to be proudly sported.[104]

This schema is valid for transclasses, as it is for all those who are stigmatized. Thus, the struggle against racism and for the recognition of equality between blacks and whites involved invoking black beauty. The 'black is beautiful' movement, born in the 1960s in the United States, aimed to break with stigmatization of the black, whose colour has negative connotations, referring to darkness, dirtiness, physical and moral ugliness, by contrast with the purity of white. It rested on the promotion of black beauty, reconciling people with their physical appearance and correcting the self-detestation that led some to lighten their skin and straighten their hair in order to ape whites.

100   Nietzsche, *On the Genealogy of Morals*, p. 22.

101   Ibid.

102   However critical of it he is, Nietzsche recognizes that a slave morality, such as Christianity's, engendered values, and ended up corrupting minds to the extent of prevailing over aristocratic morality.

103   Nietzsche, *On the Genealogy of Morals*, p. 22.

104   Erving Goffman, *Stigma: Notes on the Management of Spoiled Identity* (London: Penguin, 1990).

Similarly, the positive invocation of homosexual pride, expressed in particular in the form of the processions and parades of Gay Pride, aimed to invert the stigma and emerge from silent shame in a joyful self-display. Intended at first to commemorate the Stonewall Inn riots in June 1969, in the form of Pride and then the Christopher Street Parade, initiated by Brenda Howard (dubbed the Mother of Pride), Gay Pride arose against the demonization of homosexuality and its moral condemnation, proclaiming the equal goodness of human beings, whatever their sexual orientation. The acronym GAY furnishes one of the main slogans of the demonstrations: 'Good as You'.

In the case of the transclass, the inversion of stigma rests on a reappropriation of the past in order to bring an end to the cleavage and put the pieces back together. This reappropriation involves acceptance of one's origins and their reconfiguration, so that they appear no longer as an indelible mark of infamy but as an historical moment of self-constitution. The attempt to unify one's complexion takes the form of transforming division into integration, in two senses – integration into the new milieu and integration of the origin into the destination.

One of the first figures of self-reconciliation among transclasses consists in invoking the origin as a claim to fame. This too involves emerging from the closet, coming out, displaying one's pride: pride at belonging to the proletarian world; pride at success, which proves what its members are capable of; pride at avenging violated honour and restoring dignity. Instead of keeping quiet, the transclass makes herself the herald of the popular classes, the voice of the obscure and the forgotten, the memory of history's speechless people.

Camus thus conceives literature in the guise of testimony, in an account that restores the nobility of his people: 'Rescue this poor family from the fate of the poor, which is to disappear from history without a trace. The Speechless Ones. They were and are greater than I.'[105] This ambition to restore the grandeur of the little people, to make oneself the avenger of the oppressed, to assume their colours loud and clear by giving them a face to wrest them from the anonymity of death and the insignificance of life, is a concern widely shared by numerous transclasses. To such an extent does rehabilitating the dominated represent a kind of mandatory passage to escape shame and assert one's dignity, that it is often a leitmotif in their writing.

In this regard, Michelet provides a prototype of inversion of the stigma that warrants attention, not so much because it makes the people a genius, rather than a dirty populace, in broad strokes of crude essentialism, but because he sketches figures making it possible to pass from the ashamed transclass to the glorious transclass. Hailing from a family of peasants with a father who was a printer, he became a famous historian familiar with the fluctuations of the in-between and the division bound up with dual affiliation, as he himself confided: 'I was suffering . . . far more than any other from the deplorable divorce that some are endeavouring to produce among men, between different classes, I who combine them all within me.'[106] Although it was not his immediate objective, in *Le Peuple* he developed two fictional models of the transclass: the 'bastard' and the 'barbarian'.

To the repulsive figure of the bastard who is unaware of his origins, or conceals them in hybridization so that the race is exhausted, Michelet opposes the positive figure of the barbarian, who does not disavow them, but sweeps aside everything in his path and asserts his own vitality uninhibitedly and shamelessly. Michelet thus subverts a negative image by adopting it for his own positive purposes:

---

105 Camus, *First Man*, Appendices, p. 238.
106 Michelet, *The People*, p. 14.

Often, in these days, the rise and progress of the people are compared to the invasion of the *Barbarians*. The expression pleases me; I accept it. *Barbarians*! Yes, that is to say, full of new, living, regenerating sap. *Barbarians*, that is, travellers, marching towards the Rome of the future, going on slowly, doubtless; each generation advancing a little, halting in death; but others march forward all the same.[107]

The historian thus replaces the figure of the bastard with that of the barbarian. He detaches the term *barbarian* from its pejorative sense, attaching it to the eponymous people and giving it a new meaning. He inverts the stigma, for the barbarian ceases to be the brutal savage bereft of culture and civilization, the destructive vandal, and becomes the figure of the traveller marching to the Rome of the future. The Barbarians are a nation of conquerors without shame and full of ardour, of the race of lords who march proudly on Rome and do not give a damn about destroying an old order to impose their new values.[108] The barbarians are therefore no longer foreigners, those who do not speak a human language, who reproduce the indistinct, inarticulate song of the birds, according to the probable etymology of the word.[109] They are men who proudly advance towards a future that is collectively constructed step by step.

---

107 Ibid., p. 13. Emphasis in original.

108 It is interesting to note that a few years later Nietzsche too was to refer to the barbarian hordes, not in connection with the rise of the people, but that of aristocratic man. See Nietzsche, *On the Genealogy of Morals*: 'The noble races are the ones who, wherever they have gone, have left the concept of "barbarian" in their wake; an awareness of this is betrayed even by their highest culture . . .' (p. 26).

109 See Claude Lévi-Strauss, 'Race and History', in *Structural Anthropology 2*, transl. Monique Layton (Harmondsworth: Penguin, 1978), p. 328.

We should note here that Michelet does not view social ascent as a solitary adventure, but as an enterprise of transformation of an entire people over several generations. In his view, individual change of class must be extended into a movement of collective progress. Otherwise, the innovative energy risks lapsing into reproductive inertia and giving birth to bastards, rather than barbarians. Accordingly, he outlines the road to be followed for the first transclasses. If they do not want to decline, those who rise must be barbarians, pathfinders, displaying the precursory signs of a rediscovered pride. This implies their not confining themselves to being mere passengers who switch sides, but being pioneers marching towards the conquest of a history that destroys classes with their straitjacket of inequality and injustice. It is no accident that marching is frequently chosen as a symbol of rediscovered pride. Whether it takes the form of a parade, a demonstration, or a procession, it involves human beings standing upright, refusing to live on their knees, setting themselves in motion to shift the lines of subservience.

The two figures first delineated by Michelet are not to be understood in the form of an antinomy between negative and positive types of transclass; in the course of their career, everyone can be 'barbarian' or 'bastard' by turns. Far from representing norms, they can serve as an imaginary reference point for making one's way and walking with one's head held high. Moreover, the conquest of pride is a necessary but insufficient condition for going beyond tensions and living without alienation. In absolute terms, this affect has no more justification than shame, for there are no such things as intrinsic glory and infamy attaching to one condition, one race, one sexuality rather than another.

From being a simple antidote to shame, pride can in turn become a poison, when it becomes a hegemonic self-assertion at the expense of others. It degenerates into arrogance and

turns into the form of pride that is 'born of a man's false opinion that he is above others'.[110] In this case it is no more than
an inverted shame, in which everything becomes a reason for
election instead of abjection. Pride is proportionate to the
shame that preceded it. But when pride at success is transformed into a frantic quest for recognition, into unlimited
desire to win or to prove one's superiority and legitimacy by
accumulating wealth, culture, power, or honour, the transclass
is utterly alienated in the judgement of others. Capitalizing
incessantly, she is condemned to a Sisyphean task, prey to
what Hegel called the bad infinity of desire. Forever seeking to
prevail over others, she becomes self-important and tiresome.
What is most human is not only (as Nietzsche said) to spare
someone's shame but also to preserve them from pride.
Consequently, a free human being is a human being without
shame and without pride.

The transclass does not have to boast of her native class,
worshipping it and deferring to it excessively, any more than
she does of her social success. Such social piety is based on an
idealization of the people, and attests to a blindness sometimes verging on stupidity. This is the mistake of populist
currents, particularly workerism, which sings the praises of
the proletariat and extols its superior value, its morality and
culture, supposedly more authentic than that of the dominant
classes. The painter and sculptor Constantin Meunier thus
made himself the champion of mineworkers and the glorifica-
tion of labour.

In an issue of the journal *L'Anarchie* in 1910, Le Rétif (alias
Victor Serge) criticized the excesses this idealization leads to in
a highly sarcastic tone, equating workerism with a strange
illness bound up with distorted vision.[111] He denounces the

---

110 Spinoza, *Ethics*, Book IV, proposition 57, scholium, p. 145.
111 'Workerism? It is a strange illness from which virtually the
whole supposedly advanced intelligentsia suffers. Marxism and

habitual attitude in the most educated circles of 'admiring the prole' and devoting a whole right-thinking literature to the martyrs of labour. 'Little by little one came to imagine a worker barely corresponding to reality. He is the admirable miner of Constantin Meunier, the handsome worker with the powerful torso and proud gaze, whom one sees on socialist engravings advancing joyously towards a large purple sun . . .'.[112]

Rather than 'exalt the worker, whose lamentable lack of consciousness is the cause of universal grief, more so perhaps than the absurd rapacity of the privileged', for Le Rétif it was necessary 'to endeavour to let a bit of daylight into the appalling darkness of brains', in order to sow the seed of good harvests and enlarge the ranks of those whom he calls 'life's lovers and fighters'.[113]

The intellectual defence of a glorified people is perhaps the highest form of treason. In addition to being a form of paternalism and demagogy, it attests to ignorance of, and scorn for, an everyday reality, also marked by alienation and prejudices, which it risks replicating rather than helping to free people

---

syndicalism are incurable forms of it. An enormous number of anarchists suffer from it. It consists in a more or less serious distortion of the faculties of seeing and thinking, which makes everything working-class seem beautiful, highly useful, just as that which is not working-class is ugly, bad, useless, if not harmful. The sad idiot, slumped, alcoholic, addicted to tobacco, and suffering from tuberculosis, that is the mass of fine citizens becomes by enchantment the worker, whose "august" toil causes humanity to live and advance, whose magnanimous effort reserves a splendid future for him . . . Take care not to observe to the workerist that the so-classed proletarian is ultimately the surest support of the abominable regime of Capital and Authority, which he sustains and sanctions by military service, voting, daily labour. You will at once find yourself treated as a backward individual, with bourgeois prejudices, who understands nothing of . . . sociology.' 'Le Rétif', *L'Anarchie* 259 (24 March 1910).

112   Ibid.
113   Ibid.

from. Recognizing the dignity of the popular classes does not prevent one observing that a good proportion of them are far from being progressive when it comes to acknowledging the rights of women, homosexuals, and immigrants, or their place in society. As in the case of shame, it is therefore appropriate to distinguish healthy pride from deadly pride, and to guard against the dual idealization of class starting-point and class endpoint.

Besides, it should be noted that nostalgic valorization of the native milieu can have complex motives that attach less to pride than to a desire for compensation faced with class inequality and the injustice of conditions. If it is easier for a wealthy person to display indifference and ignore the suffering of a milieu she does not frequent, it is much trickier for a transclass to forget those she leaves behind, who have given her a leg up.[114] What agitates the transclass is not so much lived misery as the idea that others still have to suffer it, triggering surges of guilt and impotent rebellion.

Michelet thus affirms that privations, hunger, cold, and the uncertainties of the morrow never shook him. He put up with them stoically, especially the snowy day without fire or bread when everything seemed over, when 'with my frost-bitten hand I struck my oaken table . . . and felt a powerfully joyous

---

114   This is noted by Michelet: 'What should a rich man know, with all the science in the world? The very circumstance of his living an easy life causes him to be ignorant of its great and profound realities. Never investigating deeply, or with energy, he runs, and glides along, on the ice; he never penetrates, always remains on the surface; in that rapid external and superficial existence, he will reach the goal to-morrow, and will depart just as ignorant as he came' (*The People*, pp. 125–6). Michelet obviously does not mean that all wealthy people are obtuse, but that their condition does not predispose them to understand life and its inequalities. This moralizing analysis must be tempered, however, for the popular classes have no monopoly on social suffering.

impulse of youth and future prospects.' By contrast, he confesses: 'life has but one hold on me, that which I felt on the 12th of February last, about thirty years after. I found myself . . . opposite the same table. One thing smote my heart: "Thou art warm – others are cold; that is not right. Oh! who will relieve me from this cruel inequality?"'[115]

More than past misery or shame, the sense of injustice at human inequality is what can eat away at the transclass, with its train of bad consciousness and powerlessness. She suffers for others, and this is perhaps the worst of sufferings, for sometimes one bears one's own pain more easily than that of one's nearest and dearest. How to live in peace with one's conscience and not have the impression of being a traitor, a wealthy one, a monster of egotism who abandons others to their fate?

To escape Cain's eye, one has to be able to justify oneself in one's own eyes by being aware of the necessity of one's own position – necessity in the dual sense of determinism and utility; to meditate on determinism and utility in order to struggle against culpability. On the one hand, the transclass is not to blame for being where she is. Her situation is the result of combined external and internal forms of determination – and it would be mistaken to think that she could have been any different, given her history. For that, she and her environment would have had to be different from what they were.

Consequently, to conceive oneself as a miracle survivor of destiny, a lucky escapee or terrible traitor, is always to be mistaken out of ignorance of the determinism at work in non-reproduction. Guilt must therefore rebound on itself and serve as an antidote. In other words, one begins to think straight when one feels guilty about feeling guilty. On the other hand, the transclass is sometimes more precious for her

---

115 Ibid., p. 11.

milieu outside it than inside it. This is what Michelet asserts to appease his conscience on that famous 12 February: 'then, looking at my hand, the one which, from 1813, still shows the traces of the cold, I said to myself for consolation, "If you were working with the people, you would not be working for them. Come then, if you give its history to your country, I will pardon you for being happy."'[116] Reparation takes the form of writing the *History of France*, where Michelet seeks to give the people their due by making them its hero and principal protagonist. The point here is not to judge the scientific quality of the enterprise, but to understand the approach that informs it. It is clear that we are dealing with an attempt at redemption of the self and one's own people in and through the historical resurrection of those who have no history.[117]

To be able to be oneself through the other, the transclass has no alternative but to transform what crushes her into a lever, to rely on tensions, eroding the brake of guilt so that it becomes a driving force. Thus, Annie Ernaux's work results from the conversion of shame and guilt into a literary oeuvre, and exemplifies the way that a transclass manages to reconcile opposites and assume the wrench of the in-between. The quotation from Genet – 'May I venture an explanation: writing is the ultimate recourse for those who have betrayed' – highlighted in *A Man's Place*, clarifies the approach that inspires the author.[118] Moreover, this is what she confirms in *L'Écriture comme un couteau*:

---

116   Ibid., pp. 11–12.
117   Michelet wrote as follows to Eugène Noël in July 1845: 'We commoners don't conserve the history of our fathers, like the nobles do. That history of obscure virtues would often be of great interest.' Quoted in Robert Casanova, 'Introduction', in *Le Peuple* (Paris: Julliard, 1965), p. 25.
118   Ernaux, *A Man's Place*, p. 3.

I believe that this guilt is irrevocable and that, while it underlies my writing, it is also writing that most frees me from it.
The image of the 'donation' at the end of *Simple Passion* therefore applies to everything I write. I have the impression that
writing is what I can do best, in my case, in my situation as a
transfuge, as a political act and as a 'gift'.[119]

The author finds resources in the guilt that torments her, not
to move beyond it – an impossible task – but to reverse it
into a driving force. She feeds off this ambivalent affect,
which paralyzes and galvanizes by turns. Infusing itself with
it, the writing consummates and consumes it, at least partly.
In short, the book is a release. Writing emerges as a form of
reparation, donation, a way of paying one's debt. This does
not mean believing that feelings of guilt automatically haunt
all transclasses and mechanically produce sublime effects.
Annie Ernaux observes that, in her case, the sense of guilt is
complex. It is not only linked to changing social class but
also has familial, sexual, and religious roots by dint of her
strictly Catholic education.[120] She also makes it clear that,
while the act of writing is not a substitute for political
engagement, it is a political act and not a merely aesthetic
activity severed from any social determination or impact on
the real world. An author writes in a given situation – hers
and that of the world – and cannot, by who knows what
miracle, escape class determinations when her neighbours
across the landing belong to the middle or upper class.
Writing therefore implies awareness of the writer's member-
ship of a determinate class and, in its way, helps to conserve
or transform the state of the world.[121] Realizing the existence
of classes and her transclass situation orientated Annie

---

119   Ernaux, *L'Écriture comme un couteau*, p. 62.
120   Ibid., p. 63.
121   See ibid., pp. 74–5.

Ernaux towards a realistic view of the world, rather than an aestheticizing one.[122] Her oeuvre is therefore marked by this predilection for the real specific to many transclasses: 'I no longer wanted to make something beautiful first, but something real, and writing was this labour of excavation of reality: of the popular milieu of childhood, of acculturation which is also a wrenching from the original world, of female sexuality.'[123]

The question is what to do in order to grasp this reality and not betray for a second time, invalidating any attempt at reparation. This is the main thing at stake in the enterprise, and it rings out like a challenge to be taken up: 'to make' in such a way that the donation is not a poisoned chalice, with a comic-opera populace in each vignette. Annie Ernaux is fully aware of this. She knows that she is proposing to write about the dominated world while now belonging to the dominant world; that she runs the risk of failing to restore the objectively and subjectively lived reality, betraying her native class twice over – the first time involuntarily, by her educational career, and the second time deliberately, by consciously positioning herself in her choice of writing from the side of the dominant. She must therefore avoid the twofold danger of lapsing into a miserabilist account tinged with populism, or into the distanced standpoint of higher classes, who regard the 'world down below' as an alien, exotic curiosity.[124]

---

122 See ibid., pp. 76–7.

123 Ibid., p. 77. This is also observed by Richard Wright in *Black Boy* (London: Vintage, 2020): 'At the age of twelve, before I had one full year of formal schooling, I had a conception of life that no experience would ever erase, a predilection for what was real that no argument could ever gainsay, a sense of the world that was mine and mine alone, a notion as to what life meant that no education could ever alter, a conviction that the meaning of living came only when one was struggling to wring a meaning out of meaningless suffering' (p. 99).

124 See ibid., pp. 78–9.

Before publishing *Empty Cupboards* and writing *A Man's Place*, Ernaux, attracted by the literary movement of the *nouveau roman*, tried writing poems and experimental fiction, 'a kind of disembodied object, highly ambitious', in her own words.[125] This unpublished novel, written when she was twenty-two, borrowed nothing from memory and was inscribed in the culture of the dominant in line with a logic more 'bastard' than 'barbarian', so to speak. Awareness of her status as a transclass led Ernaux to invent what she calls 'the writing of distance' and to get the better of the snare of treason through the intrusion of the view of the dominated in literature. Thus, she plays with the tensions of the in-between, integrating into the narrative, with its classical literary form, words and phrases of the popular classes like *gagner malheur* (go mad), and sometimes pieces of Norman dialect whose meaning she explains to readers.[126] The text, albeit written in the enemy's language, in a formula of Genet's of which she is fond, with the linguistic tools of the dominant, can then introduce by intrusion the viewpoint of the dominated – her father, her mother, the popular classes of Yvetot and Normandy. This is where she becomes positively 'barbarian', overthrowing syntax, subverting the language in order to enable the dominated to burst onto the front of the literary stage.

This writing of distance leads her to break with the classical form of the novel and opt for a style that reconstructs the turns of phrase of colloquial language. The option of 'flat writing' imposed itself as an obvious move in the composition of *A Man's Place*:

> I realize now that a novel is out of the question. If I wish to tell
> the story of a life governed by necessity, I have no right to

---

125   Annie Ernaux, *Retour à Yvetot* (Paris: Mauconduit, 2013), p. 28.
126   Ibid., p. 33.

adopt an artistic approach, or attempt to produce something 'moving' or 'gripping'. I shall collate my father's words, tastes and mannerisms, as well as the main events of his life. In short, all the external evidence of his existence, an existence which I too shared. No lyrical reminiscences, no triumphant displays of irony. This neutral way of writing comes to me naturally. It was the same style I used when I wrote home telling my parents the latest news.[127]

Marked by verbal sobriety and economy, flat writing is an informative, factual writing that gets straight to the point without stylistic effect. It is a form of writing involving objectifying distance, without affects or miserabilist or populist coloration, without complicity or connivance with the educated reader.[128] It takes the form not so much of a narrative as a reconstruction of words heard or a salvaging of the voice of the dominated, which, without it, is destined to remain forever silent.[129]

This flat writing is the bladed weapon, the knife Ernaux needs so as not to betray. She experiences it as taking a risk, bound up in her thematic and stylistic choices alike. Aside from the books that directly grasp the reality of the dominated world, such as *A Man's Place*, *Shame* and *A Woman's Story*, Ernaux turns towards subjects treated in a bare style, without protective euphemism or lyricism, which expose her, put her in danger – for example, the account of her abortion in *Happening*, following a novelistic version in *Cleaned Out*, or her alienation in passion, in *Simple Passion*, *Getting Lost*, or *The Possession*. The perilous orientation of the work seems like a final attempt

127 Ernaux, *A Man's Place*, p. 15.
128 See Ernaux, *L'Écriture comme un couteau*, p. 34.
129 Ibid., p. 34. See also the chapter titled 'Écrire pour sauver', pp. 121–4.

to expiate guilt and subvert dominant views of the world. The desire to write something dangerous is bound up with a sense of having betrayed her native class. She experiences writing as both a form of suffering and a luxury from which she seeks to redeem herself by working with her pen, instead of her hands, to help change the view of the world by introducing the viewpoint of history's forgotten ones.[130]

By paying for it personally, she gets closer to the world of the dominated and participates in the struggle against domination in the theoretical field. It is in this inverted language, where reality regains its rights, that she makes the donation. Thus it is through the writing of the real that the stitching can be done: transcending the tear in words. This is what emerges explicitly from her statements: 'In and through the choice of this writing, I believe I am taking on and transcending the cultural tear: that of being an internal immigrant in French society.'[131]

Ernaux thus found her place through this transclass writing, haunted by passing from the dominated world to the dominant one. She takes up the in-between by inventing a language and an original socio-biographical literature. She thus casts herself as an authentic passer, who endeavours to be herself through the other. In this she has doubtless attained her objective, if we are to believe *L'Écriture comme un couteau*: 'Basically, the ultimate goal of writing, the ideal I aspire to, is to think and feel in others, as others – writers, but not only them – have thought and felt in me.'[132]

Yet this is not to be erected into a model, for each transclass, in her place, is constituted through the fluctuations and tensions of her complexion, and strives to disconnect or

---

130 Ibid., p. 52.
131 Ibid., p. 35.
132 Ibid., p. 44.

reconnect the threads, to embody it as best she can. Consequently, literature is not necessarily the royal road or obligatory passage.

Thus, this was not the trajectory Pierre Bourdieu followed to reconcile opposites, although Ernaux refers to him as decisive for her own project.[133] In his *Sketch for a Self-Analysis*, Bourdieu shows how the tensions inherent in his complexion as a transclass were expressed, and partially resolved, by reintegrating his native world into his research, through the transition from philosophy to sociology and, in particular, the rural sociology that comes last on the scale of specialisms.[134] The forced coincidence of opposites peculiar to the cleft habitus is manifest in the style and topics of his research, focused on empirical, humble objects, which he aims to examine with his undivided attention, giving them unprecedented speculative significance. Bourdieu finds his true place by displacing himself. He gradually ceases to occupy the hegemonic position inherent in philosophy, which embraces the world from the heights of the concept, and descends into fieldwork, plunges into empirical data, as indicated by his studies on Algeria, peasants in Béarn, or the world's misery. This intellectual reorientation, described as a conversion, is lived as a reappropriation of his native world, compensating for the loss of prestige consequent upon the selection of objects possessing little institutional value. Bourdieu reckons that 'the deliberate renunciation implied in this negative displacement within the hierarchies would no doubt not have been so easy if it had not been accompanied by the confused dream of a reintegration into my native world'.[135]

---

133 Ibid., p. 87.

134 As I was finishing this book, I discovered that in his latest book, *La Société comme verdict*, Didier Eribon analyses Bourdieu's career as described in *Sketch for a Self-Analysis*. Readers are referred to Part I, Chapter 3, 'Les paradoxes de la réappropriation'.

135 Bourdieu, *Sketch for a Self-Analysis*, p. 60.

To abandon philosophy is to renounce a dominant posture, to devote himself instead to ethnographic research that made it possible to reconnect with the dominated, to rediscover his own people with the tenderness and restrained emotion that surface once shame has receded. This is what emerges from a very beautiful passage in *Sketch for a Self-Analysis*, where Bourdieu describes the return to the origins after the remote detours imposed by his social trajectory:

> But, proving that the heuristic trajectory has also something of an initiatory journey about it, through total immersion and the happy reunions that accompany it, I experienced a reconciliation with things and people from which the entry into another life had imperceptibly distanced me and for which the ethnographic posture quite naturally imposed respect: childhood friends, relatives, their manners, their routines, their accent. A whole part of myself was given back to me, the very part by which I was bound to them and which distanced me from them, because I could not deny it without renouncing them, ashamed of both them and myself. The return to my origins was accompanied by a return, but a controlled return, of the repressed.[136]

The coincidence of opposites is therefore not so much a conciliation as a reconciliation with others and oneself. It takes the form of integration of the other into the self, of the ashamed part of oneself that is denied and repressed behind the class barrier. Paradoxically, however, what authorizes the reunion is the ethnographic culture acquired within the dominant world. Bolstered by the benign neutrality required of the ethnographic posture, which filters shame and compels respect for objects, research on celibacy and the peasant condition can become an encounter with oneself, a

---

136 Ibid., p. 62.

self-restitution. As in Ernaux, the research is conducted in the 'language of the enemy', but turned into its opposite, for it is no longer estranged from the native world, but proximate to it. We can understand why Bourdieu's ethnographic project is 'to do a "*Tristes Tropiques* in reverse"'.[137] Whereas Lévi-Strauss begins by getting close to remote peoples and then distancing himself on his return, Bourdieu begins by distancing himself from the people close to him, and then gets close to them and returns to them. Lévi-Strauss's research is a journey towards the other via the stranger, Bourdieu's is a journey towards the self via the familiar. The counterpart to the more exotic tropics is the more humble, more banal rural world. The one sets out from on high, uncovering the structures and kinship rules applied by the peoples of the Amazon region without their necessarily being aware of it. The other starts from below and examines behaviour on the basis of interviews and confidences from the relevant parties. Although he too diverted away from philosophy, Lévi-Strauss occupies more of an overarching position in revealing to human beings the truth of their behaviour, whereas Bourdieu attends to them and allows the dominated to speak, learning about the world's misery from them.

Over and above this contrast with Lévi-Strauss, Bourdieu's trajectory goes beyond the mere framework of an inversion, taking an original road that led him to abandon 'the heights of philosophy for the wretchedness of the *bidonville*'.[138] That is why Bourdieu does not confine himself to reproducing Lévi-Strauss in reverse, but develops a new sociology, breaking with structuralism. This rupture is manifest in 'Matrimonial Strategies in the System of Reproduction Strategies', in the transition from the model of rules to that of strategies, in the abandonment of structure for habitus,

---

137 Ibid., p. 63.
138 Ibid., p. 71.

and of system for socialized agent.[139] The investigation of Béarn is accompanied by reflexive labour that makes it possible to understand how the use of a social experience, as long as it is critical, can, by virtue of the proximity between investigator and investigated, be converted from a handicap into capital and placed in the service of scientific analysis.[140] By dint of his career as a transclass, Bourdieu gravitates towards original objects and approaches. He is living proof that he has reproduced neither the habitus of the world of the dominated, nor that of the dominant world in the strict sense, but has fashioned distinctive practices of existence and research through the conflicts of the in-between. Thus, he is a model of non-reproduction determined by his transclass complexion, by the play of contradictions that induce self-invention through the other.

Once again, this career cannot be erected into a paradigm. Not all transclasses can recognize themselves in Bourdieu's odyssey of reappropriation and his mode of return to the world of origins. The *ethos* of distance does not always translate into cleavage, retention, or ashamed rejection of the native world. Some transclasses always have the taste of childhood in their mouth, carrying with them a world that never leaves them. Consequently, it is not a question of defining mandatory phases and prescribing rules for being oneself through the other, subjecting the transclass to some kind of entrance exam. Just as there are no instruction manuals for existence, there are no transclass books of savoir vivre. Everyone is condemned to invent their freedom with others, trying to be more of a 'barbarian' than a 'bastard'. Pierre Bourdieu and Annie Ernaux are two exemplary cases of non-reproduction. But they cannot

---

139 Pierre Bourdieu, 'Matrimonial Strategies in the System of Reproduction Strategies', *Annales* 4–5 (July–October 1972), pp. 1,105–27; Bourdieu, *Sketch for a Self-Analysis*, pp. 63–4.

140 Ibid., p. 65.

be transformed into models to be emulated. They can serve as a compass, but do not represent norms. They indicate a road, but everyone marks out their own path, exploring the possibilities opened up by the in-between, in accordance with the necessity peculiar to them.

Conclusion: Complexion versus Habitus

The transclass is living proof of the existence of the mobility and plasticity of human beings, even in the most unfavourable conditions. She puts paid to an essentialist view of human beings – the belief that they are predetermined in fixed, immutable fashion – as well as an existentialist view according them the status of naturally free subjects. Non-reproduction presupposes neither the negation of determinism nor the surreptitious reintroduction of free will. It is not a self-creation of the self, but a social co-production of the native milieu and the new milieu, in as much as it only comes about with or against them. It implies that an individual, in transit between two classes, clears a path and by turns fashions, and is fashioned by, the worlds she crosses through and that cross through her. Thus, it sets in motion an interaction and cannot be reduced to the solitary career of a wilful human being.

The trajectory of transclasses is unintelligible in the absence of a conception of complexion that grasps the set of common and singular determinations intertwined in an individual, through her lived experience, her encounters, where her private and collective history intersect. This conception of complexion is based on an understanding of the interconnection of causes and the constitutive bond that defines being with others. It breaks with a substantialist conception of human beings as independent beings and invites us to avoid taking habitus as the exclusive explanatory model in accounting for social conduct. Social habitus incline human beings to reproduce the way of life of their class, and do not always make it possible to explain subtle differences. Non-reproduction runs counter to forms of social conditioning and the systems of enduring dispositions they generate. It is characterized by an aptitude for diverging from the dominant schemas and overcoming the obstacle of repetition or imprisonment in the same. Yet it does not abolish them. Rather than contradicting them, it counteracts them, and its rarity attests to the power of reproduction.

That is why analysis of complexion does not involve disqualifying social habitus but including it in a larger, more complex combinatory logic where childhood, family history, place among siblings, sexual orientation, emotional life, relations of friendship or love, are integrated into examination of the trajectory. Changing social class does not boil down to either a transfer from one class habitus to another or to swapping or transplanting them. The initial dispositions are sometimes slumbering – or, on the contrary, remain operative, are modified and recast in contact with the new milieu. It yields a reconfiguration that is not reducible to an addition of plural habitus nor their hybridization, but takes the dynamic form of a constant deconstruction and reconstruction through the tensions of transition. The transclass can only be understood in the transitional dynamic where she experiences a trans-identity and the dissolution of the personal and social self. She is declassed at the risk of being forever displaced. She is out of place, on the border between inside and outside, in an in-between that exposes her to the *fluctuatio animi*. This fluctuating posture and its variations between divergence and tearing apart are what the concept of complexion makes it possible to understand.

The existence of transclasses is in fact subject not so much to a logic of exception as one of divergence. The non-reproduction of the native social model is in no way an anomaly, which would impart a separate status, the aura of the hero, or the ostracism of Judas. Instead, it is the radicalization of the work of difference within the same, of the attempt at separation whereby everyone affirms themselves in their unique being, diverging from the prevailing models and absolute imitation. No existence is pure reproduction, for the copy is never the model; it duplicates and redoubles it, betrays it or conveys it. That is why there is necessarily a margin and some slack, however little.

Thus, any human existence might be defined by a practice of differential divergence, because it always oscillates between the two figures, minimal and maximal, of conformism and originality vis-à-vis the given norms. The transclass does not evade the rule, and her trajectory can be understood in line with the distance she introduces from the habitus of the class starting point and the class destination. She can thus be more of a 'bastard' than a 'barbarian', live divergence as a laceration and seek points of suture between the opposed milieus. Her own experience is simply an amplification of the dynamic of self-alteration facing everyone in and through the changes affecting them – a dynamic of alteration whose existential stake consists in the capacity to be other without being alienated.

But if every existence is marked by variation, immobility is simply 'a more languid motion', to quote Montaigne – a movement arrested by the presence of forces contrary to change. In this respect, social reproduction is no more of a rule or iron law than social mobility. It is not an intangible structure of societies, but the expression of a balance of forces between classes, the resultant of their opposed interests.

Analysis of the causes of non-reproduction also reveals the need to take account of the role of affects in self-constitution. The transclass is the fruit of an affective complexion; she is not a simple agent who mechanically imitates or rationally calculates a strategy. How to understand her career without an admixture of shame, desire for justice, pride, anger, and indignation? How to dispense with her pain or the joyous strength derived from amorous encounters and instances of friendship? Affect plays a decisive role, and is still too often neglected by some sociologists in the name of distrust of psychology – as if it did not form part of the social and could be reduced to an eternally pre-given character trait.[1] In the Spinozist tradition, by contrast, the affect is quintessentially social. It covers the sets of bodily and mental modifications that change our power of acting, strengthening or diminishing it. A product of the intersection of the causal power of a human being and external causes, it is the expression of inter-human relations and exchanges with the surrounding milieu. The affect relates the history of our encounter with the external world, and slots into a determinism of the interactive link. Yet it is not a question of reducing behaviour to affective types and imagining that a particular feeling automatically creates a particular effect, but of thinking a unique combination, a tangle of forms of determination.

Indeed, no determination is effective and efficacious on its own. Only by dint of intersection and cooperation can it generate effects. Taken in isolation, it is one of the possible threads of the storyline of non-reproduction, but only becomes a genuine mesh when intertwined with other determinations. Thus, the existence of alternative models, the establishment of political institutions, and economic aid may be necessary conditions, but they are not sufficient. In each instance, we have to examine the interplay of the forces at work, everyone's place in a given configuration, the singular affects that modify them and combine decisively so that they diverge from the prevalent model and commence a different social trajectory. That is why

---

1 Here we must salute the innovative approach of Frédéric Lordon, who introduces affects into the social sciences basing himself on a Spinozist anthropology of the passions. See, in particular, his *Willing Slaves of Capital: Spinoza and Marx on Desire* (2010), transl. Gabriel Ash (London/New York: Verso, 2014), and *La Société des affects* (Paris: Éditions du Seuil, 2013).

we must view this class transition in the nodal form of *complexio*, not that of a horizontal, mechanical causality.

Ultimately, we might ask whether some forms of determination are more conducive to social non-reproduction, while others by contrast represent serious handicaps. Given the actual history of societies, one would be inclined to think that the coefficient of adversity is less for a man than a woman, for a heterosexual than a homosexual, for a white than a black person; and, on this basis, imagine a scale of greater or lesser probabilities of breaking through social barriers. For example, at the summit would feature the heterosexual white man, while at the bottom we would find the homosexual black woman.

Without denying their ideological impact and real influence, it would be hasty to conclude that certain determinations, such as gender, sexual orientation, or race, play an absolutely decisive a priori role in changing social class. While it is true that, as a general rule, women encounter greater obstacles in a society largely based on male domination and the promotion of men's careers, they are not systematically disadvantaged in the context of non-reproduction, despite sexist prejudices. Certainly, boys from the popular classes receive greater encouragement to do well for themselves than girls. But they also sometimes find it more difficult to submit to the norms of the education system and often do less well than girls, in particular because the models of virility inculcated in them incline them less to be docile, leading them to assert themselves in messing around, transgression and contempt for intellectual occupations.

It is also important to take into account particular situations, such as families with only one girl or without a male descendant, where children of the female sex are the only ones who can embody their parents' aspirations. In addition, some forms of devaluation of girls can be converted into an advantage in this context. Depending on familial and social circumstances, it is not unusual, for affective or economic reasons, for parents to find it more difficult to see their son leave home than their daughter. Thus, Marie-Hélène Lafon, daughter of peasants from Cantal, who became a professor of classical literature and a writer, stresses the fact that the lot of girls, more than that of boys, is to leave, because economic changes and the primacy accorded to male inheritors in the rural world mean there is no longer room for them on the farm: 'I know I will leave because the adults around me say so in words and phrases that mark the end of a world. Daughters especially are doomed to leave and do so via school, studies, the work to be found in towns and cities; I shall do the same as all of them, I shall be the others.'[2]

Similarly, sexual orientation is not necessarily a significant factor, having an impact depending only on context. If heterosexuality appears more in line with norms and exposes people less to discrimination, it is not necessarily a determinant advantage in a transclass career. As we have seen, homosexuality can also be a social motor, in that it encourages people to escape opprobrium and display success to make people forget ignominy. We therefore need to avoid a simplistic logic of accumulation of handicaps or privileges, since the analysis of individual cases reveals that what is an obstacle in some circumstances turns into an advantage in others.

Thus, it would be wrong to think that lesbian women feature systematically at the bottom of the ladder, as homosexuality does not necessarily work to their disadvantage in all circumstances. Keeping things in proportion, they are sometimes less discriminated against in work than gay men or heterosexual women.[3] Less visible and stigmatized than male

2 Marie-Hélène Lafon, *Traversée* (Paris: Créaphis, 2013), p. 15.

3 A recent statistical study conducted by two economists, Thierry Laurent and Ferhat Mihoubi, shows that in France, all things being equal, male homosexuals recognized as such in their workplace earn 6.5 per cent less than their heterosexual male colleagues in the private sector and 5.5 per cent less in the public sector. Homosexual women are not

homosexuality, female homosexuality is frequently regarded as a less serious perversion, a temporary straying, and is not always taken seriously. This attitude, which in fact attests to a profound denial of lesbian desire, and perhaps represents the most violent form of censorship there is, has paradoxically positive effects. Less frowned upon by society, lesbian women may experience a better deal in the world of work than heterosexual women. Generally having fewer children, or receiving more help with educational tasks from their companions than their heterosexual counterparts, they take less maternity leave and absences for children's illness, and are generally more available than average. They can therefore seem like ideal employees, devoted to the firm – all the more so in that sometimes, on account of their history and sexual orientation, they want to take revenge on fate.

Finally, while adversity linked to skin colour is undeniable in most societies, exceptionally, it can be inverted into a factor of positive discrimination, by dint of the introduction of quotas or 'politically correct' arrangements seeking to reserve places for those subject to racial oppression. At the margins, calculations of petty politics based on the display of black icons or *beur* faces as alibis can foil social prognoses, preventing its systematic transformation into an ineluctable destiny.

Different forms of determination are therefore not necessarily conjoined to favour, or to prevent, social non-reproduction, and only have an impact in combination with others. While it is possible to establish a parallel between the various forms of non-reproduction, in as much as they evince a divergence from a social, racial, sexual, or gendered norm, it would

---

penalized twice over: while they are discriminated against in salary terms as women, they are not penalized for a second time on account of their sexual orientation. On the contrary, they enjoy a slight salary bonus of 2 per cent compared with heterosexual women. See Laurent and Mihoubi, 'Sexual Orientation and Wage Discrimination in France: The Hidden Side of the Rainbow', *Journal of Labour Research* 33: 4 (2012).

be mistaken to think that the battles they give rise to always go hand in hand and must be conducted in tandem. While social, feminist, homosexual, and racial struggles can converge, they are not systematically intertwined to the point of being conflated or subordinated to one another.

Attempts to unify them doubtless derive from a legitimate desire not to disperse forces and to resist all forms of oppression. But they are always menaced by hegemonic temptations, expressed in the assertion of the central, primary character of the class struggle and the desire to reduce the demands specific to women, homosexuals, blacks, and so on, to problems that will ultimately be resolved with the abolition of the capitalist system, economic equality, and the advent of a classless society.

The idea of completely absorbing feminist, homosexual, and racial struggles into the class struggle is an illusion whose effect is to mask the particular forms of discrimination to which certain categories are subject, to keep them waiting, and to replicate violence by delegitimizing and suffocating demands in the name of their secondary, subordinate character. Thus, trade unions have sometimes impeded women's struggles on the grounds that they risk harming the central battle of the working class as a whole, and that they reflect petty-bourgeois aspirations. The female Ford workers who went on strike in Dagenham in 1968 to demand equal pay with men paid the price for this. The main union and its male leaders were initially not only reluctant to support them but also collaborated with management to bring the action to an end.[4]

We have to recognize the existence of a plurality of struggles: black people, immigrants, women, homosexuals, and proletarians do not pursue the same goals in all respects. They can display solidarity and discover interconnections between their respective battles, particularly as exploited workers. But

---

4   See on this point the historical film *We Want Sex Equality (Made in Dagenham)*, dir. Nigel Cole, 2010.

they are not dealing with the same figures of domination. Not understanding this, an oppressed person in one respect can pass into the camp of the oppressors in others. The ranking of struggles, and negation of their essential character, leads to a complicit blindness to the multiplicity of forms of subjection. It is therefore not a question of choosing between them, especially given that the same individual can sometimes suffer a plurality of forms of discrimination.[5]

It is against this illusion of the single struggle with its procession of latent repression that James Baldwin cautions in his *Notes of a Native Son*: 'In the thirties, swallowing Marx whole, we discovered the Worker and realized – I should think with some relief – that the aims of the Negro and the aims of the Worker were one.'[6] For Baldwin, this theorem of the convergence of struggles, supported in particular by Richard Wright, leaves too many things unexplained and suppresses the specificity of racial discrimination, too rapidly reduced to a problem of economic exploitation:

> Finally, the relationship of the Negro to the Worker cannot be summed up, nor even greatly illuminated, by saying that their aims are one. It is true only insofar as they both desire better working conditions and useful only insofar as they unite their strength as workers to achieve these ends. Further than this we cannot in honesty go.[7]

---

5   This is likewise noted by Didier Eribon, who refuses to choose between the different struggles against the various forms of domination, for each of us is at the intersection of a plurality of collective determinations and, as a result, suffers a multiplicity of forms of subjection. In absolute terms, there is therefore no reason to prioritize fighting one of them rather than another. See Eribon, *Returning to Reims*, transl. Michael Lucey (London: Penguin, 2019), p. 236.

6   James Baldwin, *Notes of a Native Son* (London: Penguin, 2017), p. 33.

7   Ibid., p. 34.

The various forms of non-reproduction, and the battles they give rise to, can therefore interlock without excluding each other, and join forces without clashing, if they register their irreducibility. Although she can embody a figure of emancipation from a stigmatized condition, the transclass is not the future of woman, the gay or lesbian, or the black person. Nor is she the future of humanity, for the objective is not to pass through the barriers of class on one's own, but to abolish them for everyone.

Index

reproduction
  Bourdieu's theory of 1–5
  collective refusal of 64
  counterexamples 5–7
  logic of 3
  by other means 59–60
  safety valve 72
resources 14–16
ressentiment 152
revenge 66
reversion 108
revolutionaries 8
Rousseau, Jean-Jacques 51–2
rules 30–2

sacrifices 124, 125
Sartre, Jean-Paul 72, 141
Savoy 43–5
self, the 148–51
  deconstruction of the
    personal 84–9
  deconstruction of the social
    89–92
  de-substantialization 84
  illusion of 84–6, 88–9
self-assertion 72, 156–7
self-blindness 28
self-censorship 29, 104, 118
self-constitution 153
self-creation 173
self-definition 73
self-differentiation 72
self-dissociation 114
self-doubt 104, 137
self-elimination 28–9, 46

self-fashioning 141–2
self-image, and shame 131
self-made man, ideology of 8,
    23, 139–42
self-promotion 20–1
self-realization 142
self-reconciliation 153
self-satisfaction 104
sexual orientation 177, 178–9
sexual shame 62–3, 64–5
shame 53–6, 62–3, 64–5, 74,
    128–42
  definition 131
  and distorted perception
    132–3
  and evil 151
  and fear 138–9
  fuel 137–8
  and guilt 132
  imaginary of 133–7
  inverted 157
  reinforcement 138
  reversal of 151–71
  role of 128
  salutary 151
  and self-image 131
  of shame 128–30
  sources 130–2
sin 136
social advantages, acquiring 2
social ambition 144–7
social capital 1–2
social categories 81–2
social climbers 9
social condition 32